THE GIRL

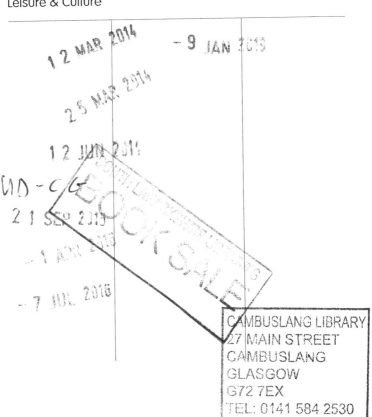

THE GIRL

A LIFE IN THE SHADOW OF ROMAN POLANSKI

SAMANTHA GEIMER

and LAWRENCE SILVER

with Judith Newman

**SIMON &
SCHUSTER**

London · New York · Sydney · Toronto · New Delhi

A CBS COMPANY

First published in Great Britain by Simon & Schuster UK Ltd, 2013
A CBS COMPANY

Designed by Dana Sloan

1 3 5 7 9 10 8 6 4 2

Simon & Schuster UK Ltd
1st Floor
222 Gray's Inn Road
London WC1X 8HB

www.simonandschuster.co.uk

Simon & Schuster Australia, Sydney
Simon & Schuster India, New Delhi

A CIP catalogue record for this book
is available from the British Library

ISBN: 978-1-47112-886-8
ISBN: 978-1-47112-950-6 (Trade Paperback)
ISBN: 978-1-47112-888-2 (ebook)

Printed and bound by CPI Group (UK) Ltd, Croydon, CR0 4YY

You see, Mr. Gittes, most men never have to face the fact that in the right time, the right place . . . they are capable of anything.

—JOHN HUSTON TO JACK NICHOLSON IN ROMAN POLANSKI'S *Chinatown*

PREFACE

*N*o. *No freakin' way. I can't do this again.*

September 27, 2009, Estes Park, Colorado. A chill in the air, snow on the mountaintops, leaves cinnamon and gold—so different from the glorious monotony of our Hawaii weather. My husband and I were in the middle of a long-anticipated vacation on the mainland—celebrating family birthdays, catching trout, watching elk rut. We were feeling particularly festive. At 6:00 AM Dave left our hotel to fish. I collapsed gratefully back into bed. At 8:15 AM the phone rang.

It was my friend Dawn. She was always looking out for me. "I have to tell you something, and you have to wake up and be ready," she said. I was instantly awake. I knew something bad had happened to her. I steeled myself.

"Roman Polanski got arrested."

Oh God. This wasn't her bad news. This was *my* bad news.

"Sam? Did you hear what I said?"

When I'm upset, I curse. I can't help it. I become a four-teen-year-old boy. "Shit shit shit shit, *what the fuck.*"

"They arrested him in Switzerland," Dawn said. "I just heard it on the news."

Sickness, panic. Need my family. Need my mother. Need a Xanax.

CNN had the story:

Oscar-winning filmmaker Roman Polanski has been arrested in Switzerland on a decades-old arrest warrant stemming from a sex charge in California, Swiss police said Sunday.

Polanski, 76, was taken into custody trying to enter Switzerland on Saturday, Zurich police said. A spokesman for the Swiss Justice Ministry said Polanski was arrested upon arrival at the airport.

He has lived in France for decades to avoid being arrested if he enters the United States and declined to appear in person to collect his Academy Award for Best Director for "The Pianist" in 2003.

The director pleaded guilty in 1977 to a single count of having unlawful sexual intercourse with a minor, acknowledging he had sex with a 13-year-old girl. But he fled the United States before he could be sentenced, and U.S. authorities have had a warrant for his arrest since 1978.

Here's a problem: This story doesn't mention the insanity that preceded his flight—the egomaniacal judge, the unconscionable uncertainty of the sentencing, the case being played out not in the courtroom, but in the media.

And here's another problem: Roman Polanski's arrest was, in a sense, my arrest. Because I am that thirteen-year-old girl.

Oh for God's sakes, it's all such ancient history, you might say. After all, it's 2013: he's eighty, I'm fifty. He is one of the most celebrated filmmakers in the world. I have a great husband, great kids, a great life. What do his problems, at this point, have to do with me?

Well, nothing. And everything.

To say that the Roman Polanski rape case was a circus is only the mildest exaggeration. For the media, there was nothing to equal its heady combination of sex, celebrity, and depravity until the O. J. Simpson trial in 1995. Just about everyone who lived through or read about this sordid chapter in Hollywood history had an opinion about the renowned director and the girl he was accused of drugging, raping, and sodomizing—me.

Opinions on the Polanski case go something like this: He was a vile pedophile whose power allowed him to escape the long arm of the law. Or: He was a troubled man whose own horrific background did not allow him to gauge the difference between a child and a young woman. And the girl? She was an innocent victim. Or, no: She was a cunning Lolita. Or, perhaps most commonly: She was a reluctant but ultimately willing player in the crazy ambitions of her stage mother, who wanted her little girl to be a star.

Who was the predator? Who was the prey? We were all suspect: Was Roman a rapist? Had my mother set up the famous director to blackmail him, using her daughter as bait? The arguments went on and on and on. Maybe the only person who lived through that time who has not weighed in on the crime and its aftermath in any significant way is . . . me. Which is why I thought it might be a good idea to tell my story.

But these thoughts only occurred to me a few months after Polanski's arrest. That day, I was in a very different frame of mind. I was thinking: Goodbye, peace. Hello, Media Nightmare. Because I knew that whenever Polanski was in the news, I would be, too.

Ask yourself this: Would you like the craziest thing that ever happened to you as a teenager broadcast and then dissected over and over on television, in the blogosphere?

Right. I didn't think so.

I called home and told my sons to unplug the phone—there were already thirty messages that had landed in the first few hours, and within the next couple of days my lawyer, Lawrence Silver, would be inundated. As much as I dreaded any time Roman Polanski was in the news, I never imagined that the appetite for this story would lead reporters to show up on Kauai. On my doorstep. My sons became prisoners in their own home. Photographers had staked out space in front of my property, sitting in their cars, waiting and drinking stale coffee. What did Rape Girl look like now? Was she fat, thin, pretty, wrinkly? Imagine how much my sons, who were then seventeen, twenty-one, and twenty-seven, enjoyed thinking about why their mom was getting this attention. Nobody likes to think about their mother getting kissed, never mind something like this.

As soon as I heard, I called Dave: "Sorry, fishing trip is over. We have problems. Come back *now*." I called Mom, who'd been staying with my aunt up the road. "What did he do now?" she asked. It didn't occur to her that his arrest, thirty-two years later, could have anything to do with *me*.

We made our way to Denver, staying overnight in a hotel near the airport. Roman's arrest was in all the newspapers and running on the ticker on the news channels. My face was on all the televisions in the lobby bar. "Everyone's staring," Dave whispered. Were they? I don't know. Maybe it was his imagination. I kept my head down. But the woman at the front desk noticed my photo in the Denver paper and upgraded us to a more secure floor. I was so grateful to that hotel, because that would be the last time I'd have any peace for the next few weeks.

In the Hawaiian airport a smattering of photographers were waiting for us. How did they even know what flight I was on? I guess all airline companies have moles. It was uncomfortable, but it was quickly over. Still, Dave and I had no choice: I couldn't go home and face the paparazzi. We slept that night at my office. A couple of days later, an article ran that said I was "clearly upset and looking tired and drawn." More like exhausted and furious.

By the time I dared to go home, most of the stalkerazzi had grumpily given up camping outside my door. I had to hand it to my sons; they helped. They monitored the cars parked in front of the house, and shouted at anyone who came by to gawk; my son Alex even went out and continually photographed one of the photographers until he left. They had to discourage their friends from confronting the photographers; my sons were having to be peacekeepers as well.

Over the next few days, we would receive more than two hundred calls, almost all from the press, and that doesn't include the ones that came to Larry's office. At the same time, my husband's cousins—the Geimer relations in California— were dealing with people knocking on their door. Geimer was an uncommon name, and reporters figured these people might have some idea where I was and what I was up to. Probably, in the minds of these media folks, I was having horrible flashbacks from decades ago. I was—but it was horrible flashbacks of *them*.

Why would all this be happening now? True, the United States could have sought Polanski's arrest and extradition worldwide at any time since 1978. But at that moment, we knew nothing. I never even realized Polanski could leave France; I had no idea he had a chalet in Switzerland and traveled, semi-covertly, in and out of several countries. At the moment all I could think was, Why would he do something so stupid? And why should I have to live through it all—again?

I called my lawyer, Larry Silver, who said, "I don't know what this is about, either. Do nothing. I'll find out."

Something, or someone, had stirred up old wounds. Maybe Steven Cooley, the Republican district attorney of Los Angeles—who, not coincidentally, was running for state attorney general—felt he had to show everyone who was the big *macher* and push for resolution in this famously unresolved case.

I suddenly recalled how uncomfortable I'd felt for many years in California, and in Los Angeles in particular. Celebrity didn't just count for a lot; to a certain segment of the population, it was *everything*. And wherever a celebrity was involved, all emotions loomed large. Adulation, yes. But retribution, too. I had this sense that the entire legal system was saying to Polanski, *You think you're better than us? Well, just wait.*

The purpose of the legal system is to punish criminals, of course, and there were many ideas about what this meant for Polanski—had he been punished enough for what he did? Did he still deserve to be held accountable? Or had the punishment been bungled so stupendously that anything further was cruel and unusual? And then there was the other purpose of the judicial system: to protect victims and protect society from criminals. So what was the sense of arresting Polanski now? Did society need to be protected from him? Did I?

Over the years, I have had bad dreams about the legal morass, the publicity, the questioning in the courtroom. But I don't think I ever dreamed about Roman or that night at Jack Nicholson's house. That doesn't mean it wasn't terrible. It was. But its terribleness didn't haunt me. Other aspects of that time did. When Roman was arrested in Switzerland, it wasn't exactly déjà vu, but it reminded me of the sense of powerlessness I had experienced as a thirteen-year-old girl. With the passing years, it had come to seem less and less likely that Roman would ever return to the States. He would live and die a celebrated director in France, where he was beloved, and I would hold on to the anonymity I cherished. And if he were to return, I assumed it would be because he'd resolved his legal problems and come back voluntarily. How could he be arrested again, thirty-two years later?

In a blink everything had returned nearly to the way it was decades before. Roman was sitting in a jail cell, and I was being hounded by the press. It was just like all those many years ago when we first met Judge Rittenband, the man who oversaw the case: we were bound again by a legal system that valued the headlines it could generate more than the effect its actions had on individuals. His rights as a defendant, my rights as a victim, were being stomped into the ground.

As the case moved again through the courts and old atrocities were revisited, my lawyer, Larry Silver, again beseeched the court to finally make the whole thing go away.

"The victim is once again the victim," he wrote. "Everyone claims that they are acting to vindicate justice, but Samantha sees no justice. Everyone insists that she owes them a story, but her story continues to be sad.

"She endures this life because a corrupt judge caused, understandably, Polanski to flee. No matter what his crime, Polanski was entitled to be treated fairly; he was not. The day Polanski fled was a sad day for American justice. Samantha should not be made to pay the price. She has been paying for a failed judicial and prosecutorial system."

"This statement makes one more demand, one more request, one more plea: Leave her alone."

. . .

Now listen: I am not naïve. If you write a book, you're not asking to be left alone. You're inviting people into your life. I know that. Welcome.

But I do have a reason. So much has been written about the Polanski case, but none of it has been written by me, the person at the center of it. So many years have gone by; it's time. I've had so many years to rage, to laugh, to marvel at what people say and why they say it. In a sense I want to take back ownership of my own story from those who've commented on it, without rebuke, for so long. Because my story is not just pure awfulness. It's crazy and sad, but yes, sometimes funny, too. It may have been messy at times, but it's my mess and I'm taking it back.

There is even, as we parents say, a teachable moment. We have what I think of as a Victim Industry in this country, an industry populated by Nancy Grace and Dr. Phil and Gloria Allred and all those who make money by manufacturing outrage. I've been part of it. If you spent years reading about yourself in the papers with the moniker "Sex Victim Girl," you'd have a lot to say about this issue, too. But for now I'll leave it at this: It is wrong to ask people to feel like victims, because once they do, they feel like victims in every area of their lives.

I made a decision: I wasn't going to be a victim of anyone

or *for* anyone. Not Roman, not the state of California, not the media. I wasn't going to be defined by what is said about me or expected from me. I was going to tell my story, my truth, through nobody else's perspective but my own.

And that is what I have done.

PART ONE

CHAPTER 1

I was born Tami Sue Nye on March 31, 1963, eight months before President Kennedy was assassinated and the ground shifted under all of us a little. I have no memory of my biological father, though he called the house once, after he'd been drinking. I'd always assumed my mother decided to change my name, partially to erase him from her life. Later I learned that's not what happened at all. It was my adoptive father, Jack Gailey, who wanted it changed. Smart girls weren't named Tami Sue. Dad wanted a smart girl.

We are from York, Pennsylvania, a factory town where the people, mostly of Pennsylvania Dutch descent, produce flooring, water turbines, and Harley-Davidsons. Astroturf was invented here; it's where York barbells are manufactured, and where the USA Weightlifting Hall of Fame has its headquarters. People born in York usually die in York.

In a town where Ozzie and Harriet were the standard-bearers for family life, we were the oddballs. Dad, who adopted me at three, was in the state legislature for twelve years and later a prominent criminal defense attorney. He was eleven years older than my mother, who was his third wife. Six feet one, bearded and bow-tied, he wore jeans and a macramé belt and a black cape in winter and was radical in his grooming— by which I mean his hair fell below his collar. A prosperous intellectual, he refused to move to a tonier area. Instead my mother, sister, and I were ensconced in an enormous *Munsters*-like rowhouse in the center of a working-class neighborhood. He held progressive views about race in a town that was deeply divided, where blacks and whites lived on separate sides of the city and you didn't dare go a few blocks in the wrong direction unless you wanted a beating. These views made him suspect. He also had left his wife and three children and married an actress—my mother. That made him suspect, too.

But then, who wouldn't fall in love with my mother? She looked like a Hitchcock blonde, but had the effervescence and charm of a car salesman. Which, in a sense, she was: In addition to the jobs she got as a spokesperson in industrial films (she could sell the hell out of a piece of linoleum), she was the Ourisman Chevrolet Girl for their Maryland dealership, declaring cheekily, "You Get Your Way at Ourisman Chevrolet." Mom was a local celebrity: She had her own glam poster, which the dealerships sold. (Recently, she got a note from someone with an attached photo—"this was my dorm room"—and the posters on the wall were her and Farrah Fawcett.) Her notoriety for those commercials extended to the Oval Office. Mandell "Mandy" Ourisman, the owner of the huge dealership and probably a big Republican donor, was at a White House event; on the receiving line President Nixon reportedly said, "That little girl who does your commercials does a good job. I'd like to meet her someday."

In all my early memories my mom is doing one of two things: fixing her makeup or telling me to go out to play. Her appearance was her calling card, and she knew it. I'm not quite sure if she was fearless, or reckless, or both; I do know she was the kind of person who didn't look back. After her first early marriage she joined a traveling rodeo, following a boyfriend who was a cowboy. It's not like she was a great rider—but she looked gorgeous on horseback, and figured she'd learn a few tricks. It beat selling ladies' shoes, which was her previous day job.

Mom didn't really have a long attention span when it came to men. She first married a local boy at seventeen when she was four months pregnant with my sister, Kim; they also had another baby, who died suddenly at five months old. They divorced shortly thereafter. Six years later, she married her second husband, Robert Nye, and had me. She divorced him when I was three and married Jack Gailey, the man I always knew as Dad. Dad could be an arrogant, superior man—because he knew he was generally the smartest person in the room—but I adored him, and he doted on me. Which is why, when I got older, I never tried to find my biological father. It felt like an insult to the man who raised me—and I'm pretty sure, given Jack's controlling nature, he didn't want me trying to find him, either.

Soon after they met, Mom and Dad were cast opposite each other in a community theater production: he was Caesar and she was Cleopatra. My mother was a romantic. Perhaps she saw a better end for her and Dad than the characters in Shaw's play.

It was obvious to me even as a child that my mother's dreams went beyond being the Ourisman Chevrolet girl. She was going to make it out of York, Pennsylvania, one way or the other. It was just a question of when. And with whom . . . because my dad had no intention of leaving his hometown.

Mine was a very happy early childhood, but at the same time it also had more than its share of chaos. We knew to go home when the streetlights came on, but that was about the extent of our monitoring. Disagreements at school were settled with ass-kickings when the teachers weren't around—girls, boys, it didn't matter; there was no such thing as "processing" or "talking it out." In my own home, my sister and I were pretty much left to our own devices, rattling around in our enormous mansion. Because my father had two law practices and my mom did dinner theater, we were largely cared for by Nana, my mother's mother. This was a little problematic, because although we loved her dearly, Nana was mentally ill. Something had happened to her when my mother was fifteen—some combination of manic depression and schizophrenia, the doctors said—and when she took her medications, she was fine.

When she didn't, she ended up in the hospital. We were never filled in on the details, but I do remember her throwing away a bunch of my father's belongings, and at one point she became convinced that the wiring in the house was making her teeth hurt, so she went into the basement and tore it out. Wiring had always been a problem for her; earlier in her life she felt her home wiring was sending her malevolent messages, so she called the FBI. We loved Nana, but she was not the most stable person you'd ever meet.

I was a smart and independent little kid, more aware than most of what was going on in the world, and desperate to learn. My sister took a picture of me holding up a sign when I was three that said I WANT TO GO TO SCHOOL, because I would cry that I couldn't yet read.

I skipped kindergarten, and once I got to school I got good grades without working too hard, but still I wasn't too happy. Being smart—particularly being a smart girl—didn't go down well in a factory town. And while later I would become perhaps too much of a people-pleaser, in the early days I wasn't good with rules and follow-through—and that's what school is. I faked a lot of stomachaches—*had* a lot of stomachaches—and given my mother's laissez-faire attitude, let's just say I didn't get an A for attendance. I never thought of myself as a child, and neither did anyone in my family. Treating me like one often backfired. I did want to please people—but even when young I had a fairly good bullshit detector. When I was four, for example, my preschool teacher alerted my mother that perhaps

I had emotional problems because I liked drawing with black crayon. That's all I needed to hear. My drawings became even more determinedly gothic.

I was a tomboy who geeked out with the guys: *Spider-Man* comics, *Star Trek,* leaping from garage roof to roof. I had no patience for girly-girls and their Easy-Bake Ovens. (Then again, I was never in doubt about my romantic interests: Donny Osmond was my man and I would stare at his poster in my bedroom, convinced his eyes were following me around the room.)

Many little girls fantasize about becoming actresses. In the early years I didn't—but then again, I think my mother dreamed that dream for me. She didn't try to get me out of my overalls and sneakers and into frilly things. Maybe that wasn't necessary, as I resembled Tatum O'Neal, who was a huge (and tomboyish) child star at the time. Mom was constantly taking pictures of us girls. She tried to get my sister an agent when she was seventeen, and she got me my first modeling job—for those Astroturf daisy doormats—when I was ten.

But ten was a memorable year for reasons other than the occasional modeling job. One day, my girlfriend Ann and I were playing in the alley behind my house when a man pulled up, said he was a cop, and asked us to go for a ride. I was skeptical. Where was his uniform? Why did he need us to come with him? But my friend wasn't able to question the authority of a grown-up. I told her to come with me. She wouldn't. I was too short to reach the latch over the back gate to get safely back into my yard, so I told her to stay put, I'd go through the front yard and unlatch the door for us. Why didn't I demand she come with me? Why didn't she just come? I don't know.

By the time I got back, she was gone. The man grabbed her, put her in the car, took her into the woods, and raped her. Then he left her, naked and shivering. She made it to someone's house, and the residents wrapped her up and called the cops.

This all happened quite quickly, and she was found later that day. But right after it happened I was warned: you don't talk about these things, you don't mention it at school, you don't let anyone know it was her or say what happened or just . . . anything. Of course, this was my friend, and one day I couldn't help asking. He hurt her, she said, and she bled. And that was it. We never mentioned it again, and within a year she moved to New York and I never saw her again.

Why wasn't I traumatized by this at the time? I think coming from the town I did, I just accepted that bad things happened and you got over it. I remember hearing about how Aunt Jane's car was stripped. I remember my mother telling me she was mugged in New York City—a knife to her neck, the mugger screaming, "Shut up or I'll cut your fucking face!" (They never caught the guy, and a few weeks later an airline stewardess had her throat slit in the same neighborhood.) One of my friends was conceived as a result of rape; another was raped in an alley by an acquaintance about six months after what happened to me.

So in later years, if you asked me what rape was—and I *was* asked, over and over—this was it: it was being abducted by a stranger. Being taken to the woods, to a dark alley. It was quick and brutal and anonymous. There was no room for seduction or gentleness, even gentle coercion, in my definition.

CHAPTER 2

It was around this time, I think, that my parents began to fight a little more frequently. Nothing out of the ordinary. It's just that my mother was doing more and more dinner theater around Pennsylvania and Maryland, and my dad did not like her being away that much. When I was ten or eleven my mother won the part of Adelaide in *Guys and Dolls*—and my father forbade her from taking it. He called the director and told him he wouldn't let her do it because it would take too much of her time.

He "allowed" her to do other theater after that, but that moment seemed a turning point. When I was ten, Mom moved to New York City—which, frankly, was not so different than her living at home, because she was gone so much. My parents were still married—but not for long.

In New York my mother met Bob Nesbitt, a fellow cast member in the off-Broadway play *Room Service*, which they were doing with Shelley Berman. Bob was tall and handsome with a great laugh—the kind of man who was easy for women to love. My mother was no exception. Soon after they met she returned to York to break the news to my dad. He was devastated—and furious. I was torn. I think a lot of kids would have hated the upheaval, hated this charming interloper, but I was never one to see things in black-and-white. I wanted my dad, but Bob was a great man. He treated me like a person, not a child. And he made my mother happy.

It was 1974. The divorce rate in the United States had doubled over ten years, and newspapers were reporting how divorcing couples were going to court for the privilege of *not* keeping their children. A California psychologist quoted in the *New York Times* declared the American family was no longer "the basic unit of our society."

I got to be an expert in traveling on my own. During the week, while Mom was in New York auditioning, I'd be back at Edgar Fahs Smith Junior High in York. Then, every other Friday I'd take the train from Baltimore to New York City's Grand Central Terminal and stay with her for the weekend in Brooklyn Heights, often crossing the bridge to explore Manhattan. New York City in 1974 was in the midst of the worst fiscal crisis in its history. It was teetering on the edge of bankruptcy, drug crime was rampant, and you couldn't even drive your car in Manhattan without being accosted by the squeegee guys with their filthy rags and outstretched hands. This was before Disney annexed Forty-Second Street; back then hookers with rainbow Afros still had the run of Times Square.

Not surprisingly, my mom didn't stay in New York long. She was getting commercial work, which paid the bills but wasn't exactly what she'd had in mind when she moved there. She had also gotten me an agent. I became increasingly ambivalent about the whole thing, so much so that as I got a little older, I'd blow off auditions. When I bothered to show up, things often went well. I got two callbacks for the starring role of the daughter in *Freaky Friday,* which ultimately went to Jodie Foster. Everyone was really excited about this, with the possible exception of me.

My mother's career still wasn't taking off, but now she was with a man who shared her ambition: to go to Hollywood and find the lives they knew they were meant to have.

In the summer of 1975, after seventh grade, Mom and Bob packed up their Ford Fairlane with me, Kim, and our dog Rocky, and headed west to Los Angeles. They'd be staying there. But for me, this was just supposed to be a summer jaunt. I'd be going home afterward to live with my father.

It didn't work out that way. At the end of the summer I flew home to live with Dad, which is where I wanted to be. But a few months later I was given a choice, or more precisely, told I had a choice: I could stay there or leave York and live with Mom in California if I wanted to. I did not. I was a daddy's girl, and besides, how many kids want to leave home and head for the unknown? My father must have thought that giving me the illusion of control over the choice would make me happy. But then I learned the truth.

He took me to a local sandwich shop, where I told him my choice was to stay with him. He said, "Look, you really are only staying here because you want to be with your friends. You have to go live with your mom." I sobbed. I could see he was glad I cried, because he didn't want me to go, either. Maybe he would have kept me, I don't know. But I think for all his progressiveness, he still felt a girl had to be with her mother. Besides, he had already moved on—he was dating, trying to make a new life. Living with an increasingly moody tween wasn't part of his plan.

That January of 1976, the first time Dad drove me to the airport, I still remember how lost I felt knowing I'd never live in York again. I couldn't stop thinking about it as I stuffed my pet rat, Odin, into my carry-on. (I was quite a good smuggler at thirteen.)

Grim as it was, York was home—and the Pacific Palisades section of Los Angeles most certainly was not. It was beautiful, sure; I lived right near the beach where, a few years later, *Baywatch* would be filmed. But to be living in a beach bungalow covered in vines—when I moved in, one sprung out of the closet, making me scream—was a shock after the solidity of York.

More shocking, of course, was the California culture. I arrived at just about the same time as the Eagles dropped *Hotel California*. ("Cool wind in my hair / warm smell of colitas rising up through the air"). I was Aerosmith and Queen; this was Joni, the Doobie Brothers, surfers and skateboarders, and a whole lot of drugs as a path to self-discovery. But with all the peace, love, and rock and roll, there was also this brooding undercurrent of violence. California, like much of the country, saw an enormous leap in violent crimes in the mid- to late 1970s. Serial killers like Herbert Mullin and Edmund Kemper, the so-called Co-ed Killer, were still fresh in everyone's mind. They would be replaced in less than a year by the even more horrific Kenneth Bianchi and Angelo Buono, aka the Hillside Strangler. In ninth grade, we were all terrified.

Mom and Bob continued to audition for acting gigs, but by the time we moved out to the San Fernando Valley in the fall of 1976, to make ends meet Bob had taken a job selling advertising at a new magazine called *Marijuana Monthly*. He and Mom smoked every night in their room—secretly, they thought—for the seven years they were together, and Mom's way of finally quitting was as quintessentially 1970s as the weed smoking itself. She was on a rafting trip in the Grand Canyon and met an English doctor who was a disciple of a swami; he came up to her and said, "You're searching, aren't you?" She replied, "Yes," and he said, "I'll give you a mantra, if you will stop smoking." Her mantra, she tells me, was "om a ram a hum madhu ram ham"—or at least she *thinks* that's what it was—and she repeated it while she paddled, all the way home, on the bus ride, on the plane—and swears it was the mantra that allowed her to quit.

Moving in with them after Christmas of 1975, I could not have felt more of an outsider, an antisocial freak in this well-to-do beach town of surfer dudes and blond bikini kittens and all their fake drama. (Pacific Palisades fight: "If you want to be friends with *me,* you can't be friends with *her.*" York fight: "I'm going to beat your ass." Which is more genuine?) It was like being on a permanent pot-infused vacation.

I don't think I can overstate the shift in attitudes toward sex in the mid- to late 1970s versus ten or even five years before. *The Joy of Sex,* published in 1972, held a place of honor in my mother's bedroom. (She never knew I read it, but naturally I did, cover to cover.) Young girls are eroticized to some extent in every culture, and at this point in time in our own culture that eroticization had become almost mainstream. Brooke Shields had posed nude for pictures when she was ten, and then, at twelve, she was starring in *Pretty Baby,* a movie about a child prostitute that probably couldn't be made today. Just one year before, Jodie Foster had raised eyebrows with her portrayal of a teenage prostitute in Martin Scorsese's *Taxi Driver. Manhattan* was Woody Allen's homage not just to New York City, but to a middle-aged man's longing for a young teenager. And of course there was that famous 1974 film where a young girl has an incestuous relationship with her father. That was *Chinatown,* directed by Roman Polanski.

The bathrooms of junior high school were filled with cigarette smoke. When we visited the homes of our friends, their parents would offer us a beer. Cocaine was just beginning to become popular, but really, that wasn't yet the drug for the kicked-back Los Angeles vibe. Like the Eagles were telling us, it was all about taking it easy, not letting the sound of our own voices drive us crazy.

I had been deeply relieved when we relocated to the Valley, a grittier place where actual people with actual jobs lived. The Valley had its celebrities, of course—in the 1940s and '50s Lucille Ball and Desi Arnaz lived out there, and Clark Gable and Carole Lombard had a love nest—but it was never known for its glamour. It was more like the prototypical sparkling suburb. The Brady Bunch allegedly lived there. And later, the Kardashians. It would be a few years before the Valley Girl would become the iconic American symbol for girls addicted to shopping, long nails, and fame.

Gradually I'd become more interested in acting: When you're a kid living in Los Angeles, being an actor seems like a perfectly reasonable career goal, shared by half the people you know. My little room was papered with posters of Marilyn Monroe (plan A) and Bette Midler (plan B). At home in York my father's influence prevailed, and I was going to be a brainiac of some sort, perhaps an attorney. Here in Southern California, none of that mattered much. I was cute. I had the head shots. I was going out on auditions and some callbacks. My mother drove me east on the 101 to an office building in West Hollywood. A casting agent would ask me to give off a look—perky! fresh!—and I'd try to oblige. (Carroll O'Connor from *All in the Family* noticed me in a hallway one day wearing a short top. He poked me in my middle and teased, "Nice belly button.")

I wanted to be cheerful about the auditions and the acting classes and all the *work* that seemed to go into chasing the brass ring. But I was still quite unhappy. I felt entirely unmoored. My parents let me entertain the illusion that I was in control of my life, when in fact I controlled nothing. I was just marking time at Hughes Junior High in Woodland Hills. When I wasn't gathered with my girlfriends trying to suss out which teachers were drunk or high ("Did you smell his breath?" "Did you see her eyes?") I'd be daydreaming about change: that Mom would land a big part, or that all the acting and gym and dance classes she drove me to in our big ol' ugly brown Nissan Maxima would lead somewhere. Did I have what it takes to make it in show business? Probably not. I liked the idea of fame much more than the idea of work.

So I was not a pleasant teen. I mean, I tried, I really did. But the message I conveyed to my family in every look and deed was "Why did you make me come here? I hate this place, and I hate you." On the other hand—well, the writer J. B. Priestley had a good point: "Like its politicians and its wars, society has the teenagers it deserves."

CHAPTER 3

One day, Roman Polanski appeared at our door.

Okay, it wasn't exactly like that. But close. What really happened was this: My sister, Kim, was dating a guy named Henri Sera, a minor film producer who'd visited the house a few times. He knew my mother was in the business, and invited her to a party at Top of the Rocks, a watering hole on Sunset Boulevard. It was an impressive gathering: Diana Ross was there, and Warren Beatty. Mom said hello to Roman, chatted a bit; he made a slightly off-color joke involving sex and tiger balm, and she laughed politely. That was it. A few weeks later, Henri called to say Roman was interviewing young American girls for a photo shoot that he was in the process of doing for *Vogue Paris*. I was asked if he could come and see me, and I said yes. I never thought about dressing up, and my mom didn't make me. I was in jeans, sneakers, an unmemorable shirt, and a baseball cap—with my pet cockatiel perched on it. That was his favorite spot.

In a few years, I would get to know a great deal about this brooding, pursed-lip little man. There was, of course, his horrific childhood. He was born Rajmund Roman Thierry Polański, in Paris in 1933 to Polish Jews, and in 1937 his parents made the tragic mistake of moving back to Poland, shortly before World War II began. When Germany invaded Poland in 1939, they were sent to the Krakow ghetto, and his parents were ultimately sent to concentration camps—his mother to Auschwitz, where she was killed, and his father to Mauthausen-Gusen in Austria, where he survived. Roman saw his father captured and marched off to the camp. When he tried to catch up with him, his father, frightened his son would be captured, shouted at him to "shove off." Polanski managed to escape the ghetto himself at eight through a hole in the fence. Because he didn't look Jewish, he was sometimes sheltered by Catholic families, sometimes tossed out to wander the countryside. On several occasions he was beaten; he still has a metal plate in his head from his skull being broken. He often had to steal his own food. That was his life until he was twelve, when he was miraculously reunited with his father after the war. His father had remarried, a woman who at first resented Roman, and they lived uneasily together until he was accepted at film school. His relationship with his father never completely recovered.

Really, he had no one.

But then, the extraordinary trajectory of success. He eventually got into acting as a teenager, and made his first movie—*Knife in the Water*—in Poland in 1962. It was a deeply uncomfortable film about the sexual tension between a bored married couple and a hitchhiker they pick up, and was nominated for Best Foreign Language Film that year. He moved to the United States and went on to direct some of the darkest, most extraordinary movies of our time: *Rosemary's Baby, Repulsion, Macbeth,* and, a few years before we met, the movie that was to be nominated for eleven Academy Awards, *Chinatown.* But even his post-Holocaust life as a celebrated director was marred by the most unspeakable of tragedies: in 1969 his pregnant wife, Sharon Tate—allegedly the first woman he had a real, lasting, fulfilling relationship with—was brutally murdered in their home, along with four others, in one of the infamous Charles Manson killings.

When I met him in February 1977, I knew nothing of this. I had seen *Chinatown* and didn't like it. I thought it was both brutal and boring. (Of course, if I had known he'd directed and starred in my favorite movie at the time, *The Fearless Vampire Killers,* I would have been starry-eyed.) And my mother and Bob, despite being in the business, weren't exactly film historians. They knew about the Tate murders, so that an air of tragedy hung over him always. They also knew he was powerful and famous and could do things for all of us. In other words, they were pretty much like every other unsophisticated aspiring actor in Hollywood.

· · ·

Polanski sat down in the living room and explained what he wanted to do. A French edition of *Vogue* magazine was looking to do a story on the differences between American girls and French girls—exactly why is a little vague, but it seemed perfectly plausible at the time—and he needed to find the right American girls. He showed my mother and Bob a beautiful spread he'd done with Nastassja Kinski in the Seychelles for a summer issue of *Vogue Paris*. The theme was "pirates" and it involved the beach, swords, buried treasure, and Kinski as the captured princess in some kind of medieval golden dress. Whether or not he was having a sexual relationship with Kinski then, when she was still fourteen, is a matter open to debate, but he did shortly thereafter. What isn't debatable is that she was so exquisite in the photos she took your breath away. She also seemed so exotic, so sultry, so knowingly sexual. In a few years Richard Avedon would make the famous image of her wrapped in a boa constrictor, and I always imagine the boa was annoyed at being upstaged.

Anyway, there were these extraordinary images of an international beauty. And then there was me, a thirteen-year-old kid in jeans and sneakers, barely developed, wearing a bird.

I was by all accounts, including my own, a very pleasant but unexceptional-looking girl. My eyes suggested no particular mystery—they were bright, but that was all. I had a roundish face, a slightly pug nose, lips that were cherry red without the benefit of Bonne Bell Lip Smackers. My hair was short, and

I wasn't quite pulling off the feathered Valley Girl cut. My voice was surprisingly husky—not Cathy Moriarty sexy, just husky. No one could ever say I slinked into a room. I sort of galumphed.

Looking back on it, I still marvel that he didn't turn on his heel and walk out the door. Was he really looking for pre-pubescent girls for a photo shoot, or was the photo shoot a good excuse? After all, Roman Polanski didn't have to work hard to get beautiful women. But maybe beauty wasn't always the point. Maybe for a man who had lived through what no one should ever have to live through, and survived, maybe extreme youth was some sort of life force. And maybe he felt he needed it.

Of course, at that moment, I was thinking nothing like this. Mostly I was thinking: Ew, there's this guy who's like my size and sort of looks like a ferret. But he's super-powerful and he wants to photograph me. *Me!* And look how happy Mom and Bob look. They were sitting upright, leaning in to him a little, listening happily.

As he showed these photos of jaw-dropping beauties in *Vogue*—girls on beaches, in fields, dressed in backless evening gowns—and explained his American teenager versus French teenager storyline, I don't know how I stopped myself from laughing out loud. I really didn't have any sense that he was checking me out, either, although certainly he must have been making *some* sort of calculation. This was boring. I wanted out.

I introduced Roman to my cockatiel, which failed to charm, and then exited to my room, my record player, and the over-the-top theatricality of Aerosmith:

Leaving the things that are real behind
Leaving the things that you love from mind

. . .

A few days later Polanski returned, clutching a small black camera. My mom gently suggested she should come along on the shoot. There was a long pause. No, Roman said, her presence might make me uncomfortable and unable to relax in front of the camera. She didn't fight him; there were already stories about Brooke Shields's crazy controlling stage mother, and she certainly didn't want to be *that*.

Roman and I drove in silence to the top of our one-block street, Flanco Road, then walked up the hill where on many evenings locals would walk their dogs, bike, or lie on the patchy grass. At night, you could check out the lights in the Valley, To-panga Canyon, and Mulholland Drive; look up and you could search for the Milky Way through the San Fernando haze.

It was late afternoon, a couple of hours after school let out. Warm, not too breezy, with a couple of hours of light ahead of us. This was the test shoot. From this he could determine if I was the right girl for the French magazine.

We stopped at a spot on the hill not fully hidden by the tall grass and he started taking my picture. I had brought two tops with me, and after one roll of film, he asked me to change into my other shirt. I turned my back to change, and was surprised that I still heard the click of the shutter. Why was he still taking pictures? Wasn't it obvious I wasn't ready? As I was changing he asked me to turn toward him, and he began giving me directions, quietly. Smile, don't smile, look at me, bite your lip, look up, turn to your left, look back at me. He was utterly focused, not on me but on getting the shot right. There was no chitchat. No playfulness. But that was okay.

"This is not working," he said. "I'm just not seeing it."

I tried again. I was used to hearing nothing but praise from photographers—either because I was *just so awesome* (my thirteen-year-old brain said) or because the photographers were being paid to take head shots and wanted to make me happy. Although he wasn't exactly mad at me, I knew I wasn't quite nailing it. I could tell he was a little exasperated when I tried to look sexy, biting my lip. The more "off" I was, the more I tried. I thought I could read him: *Give me what I want, or someone else will.*

We walked up to the top of the hill. When he asked me to take my top off altogether, I felt I had to rise to the challenge. Sure, my breasts were so small I could still wear undershirts, and sure my mother would disapprove, but this was my break. If I eventually got into the magazine—well, I'd have clothes on. Besides, I was a professional. Sure, no problem. I'll take off my top.

"Just like that," he said. "Turn." He snapped away. Then I got my blouse back on as quickly as I could. I didn't think much about it. It was all a waste of time. These pictures weren't going to be used. *Vogue* didn't have naked girls in it, like *Playboy*. Of course, this was for France. Maybe it's different in France.

The next thing I knew, I was topless again. "Put your hands on your hips now," he said. He looked a little happier. I was getting cold. A dirt biker zipped by, and Roman looked from the biker to me. "Is that bothering you?" he asked. "No," I said. I was a professional. Besides, breasts are beautiful; that's what *The Joy of Sex* said, and I thought so. It's just that I didn't have them, not really. But haven't other girls my age posed like this? Brooke Shields, or maybe Jodie Foster, she was in that *Taxi Driver* movie and, oh, I don't know, *plenty* of others.

Finally we were done, and headed back to the house, the sun setting behind us. The pollution above the Valley streaked the sky in sherbet orange and pink. It was cold, and I wished I'd brought a sweater. Had this gone well? I tried to convince myself it had. That's what I'd tell my mom. It was fine. Totally fine.

And it must have gone well enough, because although he didn't say anything to me, Roman called my mom and arranged for a second session. I was going to get my shot. Whatever I did up on that hill, it might put me on the map. My family would be stoked.

CHAPTER 4

It just happened. Have you ever heard yourself say that? How often is it true? When we do something shameful, is it more often intent or opportunity? I've asked myself that question over the years about Roman Polanski. Was *I* something that "just happened"?

On March 10, my ticket to stardom showed up again. He was dressed casually but neatly in tan slacks and a crisp pin-striped shirt with the wide collars that were the fashion of the times. He wore ankle boots with heels, and they gave his walk a certain swagger. Or maybe that's just how he walked. He was neither brusque nor ingratiating; just somewhat thoughtful and abstracted. His cologne was a little too strong. He wanted to shoot me for the magazine! Sure, the last time was super-uncomfortable, but that was the price of fame. I may have been thirteen, but I wasn't a moron. Didn't I realize that everyone had to make some sacrifices for their art? And if my sacrifice was that I took off my shirt, well, how hard was that?

Everyone was excited for me, but even though I'd said nothing about the last photo shoot, my mother sensed my discomfort. I suggested to my mom that my friend Terri go with me. Terri, who was hanging out at my house that day, was my closest friend at the time, a sweet girl from a religiously strict Catholic family, so different from mine. She seemed like a good companion for this.

But Roman was in a rush. He said, "Let's go. All the light is going to go down. Hurry up. Get your clothes." So I did, with him helping me select them. Jeans, a white blouse, a rugby shirt, a plain blue dress. We all headed out, and as we walked to his car, Terri asked how long the shoot would be, because she needed to be home by a certain hour, and Polanski warned her that it might take a while, so maybe she shouldn't come. She shrugged and headed home on her bike. I wanted her to come with us, mostly because I was uncomfortable with this adult and thought it would be more fun to have a friend, not because I was scared or anxious. My mother thought the three of us had gone together.

Roman negotiated the rolling bends on Mulholland Drive in a steel-gray rented Mercedes, on our way to . . . someone's house. I didn't know where, but it didn't matter. I sat beside him in the front passenger seat, glimpses of the canyon rushing by. It was a lovely day for my big break.

First, we stopped at the home of a brunette Englishwoman with feline features and perfect full lips—Jacqueline Bisset, I was told. I didn't know who she was, but she was very nice and offered me a glass of wine. I said no. Later, she said she was appalled she had offered liquor to a minor—that she hadn't known my real age. If you look at the photos from the time that seems implausible, but then again, maybe she just assumed Roman wouldn't be palling around with a thirteen-year-old. Even *I* thought it was a little odd that someone who didn't know me offered me wine, but at that time adults were so eager to be seen as "cool" to kids that they often treated them as small adults. I'd been offered beer or wine at my parents' friends' houses before. He took a few photos of me at Jacqueline's house—pretty, feminine, maybe just the tiniest bit risqué—and continued to worry about losing the light, so he said we would go to his friend Jack Nicholson's place. Back in the car, we talked a little.

"Do you have a boyfriend?" he asked.

I looked out the window. "Yes," I said.

That was a lie. I *had* had a boyfriend, sort of. He had just broken up with me. Steve was my first serious boyfriend; we had dated for a few months. He didn't smoke or drink because he was really into karate, and wanted to be disciplined. He drove a Camaro, which impressed everyone at my school. I was crazy about him, but he dumped me because I was thirteen and he was seventeen, and he didn't think he should be fooling around with someone that young. We did fool around, though.

"Have you ever had sex?"

That was an odd question. I replied yes. It was true, and I did not want him to think of me as a child.

"How many times?"

"Twice," I said. That too was a lie. There had been one time. It hadn't been particularly memorable; for me, at thirteen, it had been more like—well, one of those things you check off your to-do list. But I didn't want to appear naïve. If you tell someone you've had sex only once, you sound prudish and ridiculous. Twice was so much better.

Roman stopped asking questions.

The conversation turned to other things, and I relaxed and forgot all about it. We continued through Mulholland Canyon, discussing photographs. I told him about a *Playboy* cover I'd seen. My ex-boyfriend Steve had showed it to me. It was a girl in a high-cut wetsuit, unzipped very low, coming out of the surf in front of a beautiful sunset. See, if he knew I had seen *Playboy* before, he'd understand that I was quite mature. I'm not bothered by these things. I'm practically French!

The road we were on seemed familiar. I'd taken some acting classes up here, and for fun, Mom and I liked to drive around here on a Sunday. So pretty above the Valley: you get glimpses of the mountains, the houses where the stars live. Mom liked to point out the stars' houses on our drives: *Hey, Loni Anderson lives there! Marlon Brando's over there!* This was my first time actually going into the house of a movie star, though. Not that I cared much about Jack Nicholson. Yeah, he was a good actor (I'd seen him in *Chinatown*), but I wished we were going to the house of Dom DeLuise, say, or Roddy McDowall. The house of *The Planet of the Apes* guy! Now *that* would be cool.

But this was good, too.

The house wasn't huge or fancy, but it had this big redwood deck with a pool in the back, and a view of the mountains. An olive-skinned woman met us at the door with two dogs, and she and Roman chatted for a bit. Her name was Helen, and she was the housekeeper. Jack Nicholson wasn't around, which I thought wasn't a big deal. I glanced around the living room. There was lots of wood—a guy definitely lived here—and the shelves were crowded with photos and mementos.

Roman and Helen kept chatting while I walked around, trying to pretend I was interested in the house. Finally Roman turned to me. "Are you thirsty?" he asked, as we all walk into the kitchen.

He opens Nicholson's fridge, and it's jammed with juices and sodas and wines. He pulls out a champagne bottle and asks me, "Should I open it?"

"I don't care," I say.

"Is it all right?" he asks the housekeeper, and she pulls out three glasses.

They have a few sips and chat a little more as Roman begins to fiddle with his camera. Helen says she's going out. I'm glad Roman finally wants to get started. He says he wants to catch the last of the light, so we go outside. The sun is just setting over the Hollywood Hills, and I am trying my best to follow his directions. But he looks irritated. Is it me? Is it the light? Well, part of it must be the light, because he doesn't just give up altogether. We go back into the living room.

Roman hands me a glass of champagne as I stand by this antique brass lamp, willing myself to be beautiful. The champagne tastes nice. He suggests I take my blouse off. Ummm, okay. I don't need to take off my bra, because I am not wearing one. The truth is, I don't need one. I really wish I had boobs, so I have kept buying myself training bras, hoping the bras will train them to grow. But no such luck yet. Oh well, better not to think of that now. I take another sip of champagne. Roman seems more pleased. Hey, look at me! I'm really modeling now. I've seen so many off-the-shoulder shots in magazines where the girl seems to be naked, but you don't see anything. That's what he's doing, I bet. I must have good shoulders.

"Should I drink the champagne or just pretend?"

"Yes, drink it. Hold the glass to your lips. Now lower it. Sip. Look at me. Look over there. Sip a little."

I drink. He refills my glass. I drink more. He keeps refilling, but I try to pace myself. I also try to follow his directions and do a good job. And then we are done with the photos at that spot and he tells me to change my clothes.

I put on the long blue dress with the long sleeves. He walks away to put in a new roll of film, I think. It's not comfortable being in front of a doctor half naked, never mind a photographer, so when he doesn't stay to watch me change, I can't help but feel better. Still, I try not to think anything of it. This is my job, I remind myself. I am a professional, and this is what professionals do.

Next we go into the kitchen. He refills my glass. I'm perched on the kitchen counter, licking an ice cube, my tongue sticking out, and he's clicking away. I'm aware I have a little buzz going. If I don't think about it too hard, it's kind of fun, this playacting.

I can be a sex kitten like the girls in *Cosmo* too.

He shoots some more photos, and by the time we're done in the kitchen, I've downed another glass of champagne. He pours again. My glass never gets empty. He's a good host, too, I guess.

"Let's take some photos in the Jacuzzi," Roman says.

Whatever! That sounds fine to me. He suggests I call Mom first, and that's fine with me, too. He says he doesn't want her to worry.

"Are you all right?" Mom says.

"Uh-huh."

"Terri ended up not coming with us," I tell her.

"Do you want me to come pick you up?"

She sounds a little nervous or something. "No. It's fine," I say. I am feeling pretty fine at that point, enjoying the modeling more than the first time or earlier. Roman seems increasingly pleased with me. At least he isn't scowling. And he wants more photos. Finally, I am getting it right.

He gets on the phone with my mother and tells her we're at Jack Nicholson's house up in Mulholland Canyon, not very far. It's already dark, but he'll bring me home soon. Having reassured her, they hang up.

There's a little bathroom that has a door opening out to the side of the house where the Jacuzzi is, and I go in there to undress. I don't have a bathing suit, so I figure I'll go in with just my panties and once I'm in, I can get in deep enough so that I'm covered by the bubbles. I knot a towel around me.

He comes up behind me and walks past me toward the door, then he stops at the sink. He's holding this little box. It's a small yellow rectangle that you can see through. He's holding this pill broken into three parts. He asks me, "Is this a Quaalude?" and I say, "Yes." I don't know why he has asked me that. Maybe he wants to see how much I know. And I *do* know, because I've seen them in magazines. They say Rorer 714. People around the Valley wear T-shirts with "Captain Quaalude" on them. They are sedatives and muscle relaxers. They are also popular sex drugs, reputed to increase arousal.

"Do you think I'll be able to drive if I take one?"

Why is he asking me? I wonder. I mean, I know what they are. But first of all, I don't drive, so I have no idea what it takes to drive, and second of all, I really don't know what Quaaludes do. What *do* they do?

"Do you want part of one?" he asks. First I say no. Then he asks me if I've ever had one. I say I have. This is a lie. But I think, If I say I have, then I'm someone who knows what she's saying no to. I've tried them, don't like them—that's cool, right?

Then he asks again. And then . . . Oh, I don't know. He wants me to. *How can I say no?*

So then I say yes.

I gulp a third of a pill with more champagne. Eh, this is fine. Not even half a pill.

Though . . . shit. Champagne, pill. I really should have had something to eat today. Who was that girl in New Jersey? Karen Ann Quinby—no, Quinlan. Karen Ann Quinlan. She's been in the papers recently. Went to a party, took some pills and liquor, ended up in a coma. Her parents took her off the respirator but she just lay there, not able to move but not able to die. That was horrible. I begin to get a little scared. I'm relaxed—too relaxed—and I just feel like lying down on the kitchen floor and resting, maybe permanently. My muscles are liquid but my heart is beating. What if I become Coma Girl?

Okay, eat something—that'll help.

Nothing in the fridge besides booze and soda, but there are some crackers on a plate on the counter. I scarf those down. I can't find anything else. Okay, I'm just overreacting. This will be fine. Fine.

"Samantha."

I hear him calling from outside, by the Jacuzzi. It's dark out but there are some small house lights and ground lights, and the Jacuzzi itself has a bright light in it. It looks so wild, with the bright lights making the foaming water a kind of incandescent white.

He asks me to get in the Jacuzzi and I'm in just my panties and he says, "You should take your panties off."

Oh no. But, well, okay, fine. There must be a reason. The panties are dark, kind of rust-colored, maybe they'll show through the water and mess up the shot. He knows what he's doing.

Wait, how did I get here again? Let me think back. Such excitement. Roman Polanski's coming over and he wants to shoot me for a French magazine and Henri's his friend and Kim told Mom and Mom told me, and Mom and Bob say it's all so amazing and I'm like, Okay, I'll go to my room now with my pet bird and think about it. I don't know. But then again, I want to be Marilyn Monroe. What would she do? She'd be beautiful and free in the bubbles. So let's climb that hill, and who cares about the dirt-biker guy, and you want my shirt? Here, and I had sex twice, hasn't everybody, so yeah, champagne and 'lude, that's how it's done, take my panties, too.

I don't know. I get in. I've got nothing on.

I've got my champagne glass, so I pose for the camera. The Jacuzzi is nice, but it's pretty deep. After a few more shots, he gives up. "This is no good, there's not enough light." He puts his camera down and says he's getting in.

He's getting in?

I'm fine with taking off my top, I'm fine that he doesn't care about anything I have to say, and the way he acts all indifferent to me, and I can even deal with spending all this time with him because everyone tells me he's a great artist. But . . . this? No. He is a forty-three-year-old man with wet lips. He doesn't even like me.

He takes off his tan pants and sweater. Then he removes his briefs. I look away, and I don't look back up until I am sure he is in the water. I really don't want to see anything. If I don't see, I won't remember. He goes to the deep end of the Jacuzzi. I'm in the shallow end. "Come here," he says.

I want out. Now. How fucking stupid could I be? It's a hard thought to hold on to. The water is hot, and steam is rising into the night, and there's that Jacuzzi smell, sort of clean, sort of dirty. I'm a thousand miles from anywhere, and all in all, I don't think the crackers helped much.

"Come here, I want you to feel something," he says.

I knew this wasn't right. But I don't know what to do, so I tiptoe over, my head just above water. He pulls me a little closer by the waist and helps hold me up a little and moves me above one of the jets so I can feel the bubbles tickling up between my legs.

"You see? Doesn't that feel good?"

There's nothing good about it, but I know what he's getting at.

"Uh, yeah," I say. Why don't I say, "No"? Why don't I say, "Don't touch me"? I don't have the wall behind me anymore. It's just me and him in the water and the steam and the bubbles.

Then everything hits at once: the steam, the heat, the alcohol, the pill, and the panic. Have you ever been touched in a way that made you want to jump right out of your skin? This man had a reputation as a great lover. The problem is, he was not *my* great lover. I could have been any girl—as long as I was female, and as long as I was young.

My chest tightens. "I can't breathe in here. I have asthma," I say. Why did I say this? I didn't even know anyone with asthma, but I just said it. I try backing away, but he holds me firmly.

But seeing I am not happy, he suggests I jump in the pool, that it will cool me down. I don't want to do this. I really, really don't want to do this. I dip my toe in, and he says, "See? It's not cold." So I dive in and zoom to the other side. Then I jump out, grab a towel that is nearby, run to the bathroom, and put on my panties that are in there. He follows me. "How is your asthma?" he asks gently. His voice is soft, wheedling.

"I need to go home and take my medicine," I say. I'm really glad he doesn't ask me what the medication is for asthma, because I have no clue what it is and then I'll be in trouble. He says offhandedly, "Yeah, I'll take you home soon."

Then he tells me to go into the other room and lie down. "No, I have to go home," I say, but he takes me by the shoulders and walks me to the bedroom, and sits me on a large red velvet couch. He asks if I'm okay. "No, I am not okay," I say. "I better go home *now*."

He assures me I'll get better.

He holds my arms at my sides and kisses me, and I say, "No, come on," but between the pill and the champagne it's like my own voice is very far away. He's kissing my face and feeling my breasts and he asks me again if I like it, does it feel good. I say nothing, but he's a guy who makes movies, so I imagine he's filling in the dialogue for himself. *You're making me do this and now you want me to tell you I like it, too? It's not like you're going to talk me into liking this.*

Then he goes down on me. I know what this is, of course, because I've read about it, but have never actually had someone do it to me. He asks if it feels good, which it does—and that, in itself, is awful. I don't want this, my mind recoils, but my body is betraying me.

And that's when I check out. I go far, far away. There is a sense of complete and utter emptiness. *Oh, just my body. I'm not really in here. Okay. I see.*

He keeps murmuring something, and he is trying to make it nice for me, I know, but it is not nice and everything is blurring and I feel dizzy and the room is so dark. But I don't fight. Why fight? All he wants to do is have an orgasm, this little spasm that makes the world go 'round. I made the decision to just let him do it, how bad can it be, it's just sex. He doesn't want to hurt me. He just wants to do it. And that will be that. It's not like I am a real person to him, or for that matter that he is real to me. We are both playing our parts.

Intercourse is such a funny word for it, sometimes. Intercourse: "a communication between individuals." But what about when there's absolutely no communication at all? He's this old guy. He keeps asking me if I like it. Then he has a thought.

"Are you on the pill?" he asks me.

"No."

"When was your last period?"

I wish he'd shut up and just do it. I'm trying to pretend I'm not there, and he's asking me questions. And how do you expect me to answer anything? It's dark and I'm high, and I'm in a house I've never been in, alone in the blackness with this stranger. Would you please just stop talking?

"I don't know. A week or two, I can't be sure."

"Come on! You have to remember this." He is a little impatient, hoping I'll remember fast. This isn't about pleasing me anymore. At the time I have no idea why he is asking. It is only later I think, Oh, I guess he thought I was one of those girls who wanted to trap him.

"I don't know," I say truthfully. "I just don't know."

"I won't come inside you then."

Then he says something totally confusing to me: "Would you want me to go through your back?"

I say, "No," but I don't know what he is asking anyway. I just know that even though I've said no, I'll do pretty much anything to get this over with. When it happened, I still wasn't sure quite what to think. I was just like, Wait, was that my butt? Do people actually do that?

And then: done. I think. But at that very moment, there is a knock on the bedroom door.

"Roman, are you in there?" A woman's voice. I don't see her, but it's not the same woman who let us in at first. Roman quickly covers himself and gets up to answer the door. A wave of relief washes over me. Okay, now I can leave.

He cracks open the door. The woman sounds annoyed, I think, but I'm not sure. I get off the couch and grab my panties. He tells her we just got out of the Jacuzzi and we're getting dressed, and we'll be right out.

But . . . not so fast. He puts his hands on my shoulders and steers me back to the couch. Wait, he's not done? I'm confused. I think I feel . . . wetness back there. But maybe not. He gently removes my panties again. Now there's someone in the house, so should I resist and head for the woman who knocked? But I'm high, and just want to get out of here. He is not rough, and I'm not even afraid anymore. I don't even care sure what he's doing at this point, because I'm squeezing my eyes shut and it's pitch black and, well, since I was a little kid I've always been a little afraid of the dark. Home . . . I just want to get *home*.

He gets up, and so do I. I leave the room, blinking, happy to be out of that blackness. How long had I been in there? Time seemed to be playing games with me. It felt like an hour. In reality it was more like ten minutes. I go to the bathroom to clean up and I put on my panties and start scrounging for my clothes once more. I comb my hair. I'm going home soon.

He asks me to wait for him before going outside, but I don't. I mean, yes, I have to wait. He's my ride home. But I'm in a rush to get out of that house. What did he think we'd do—lie around? Talk?

I had all my extra clothes in my arms so I headed for the front door to go to the car. I didn't want to meet the woman. I wasn't sure if I could act normal. I just wanted to flee and hoped she wouldn't see me. But she did, and I heard a voice in the kitchen say, "Hello." I mumbled "Hi" or "Bye" back as I walked by the kitchen to the front door and the outside. I glanced at her; she was gorgeous and sloe-eyed, with thick black hair and a face that was all planes and angles. Didn't this woman think it was weird, her friend Roman coming here with a kid? Did this happen every day? I tucked my head down and slunk out; our eyes never met.

Leaving the house, I had only a vague sense of what time it was. The buzz of traffic was still too strong for it to be anywhere close to midnight.

I walked to the car and got into the front passenger seat. I was happy to know I was going to be home soon. But I was exhausted, overwhelmed, and, although I didn't realize it, pretty loaded. I started to cry, with both relief and anger. I knew something bad had happened, and that I had done some dumb things, but I was going to be okay. After all, he was this famous man—and famously experienced lover—who hadn't wanted to hurt me; he even wanted me to feel pleasure. Later I heard that older men seducing young girls was quite the thing where he came from—that in his mind, I should probably be grateful for his experience, his technique.

But I wasn't European. I was an American girl. And I wasn't feeling grateful.

Then, the self-recrimination began. God, why would I take that pill? What was I thinking? And why was I posing topless? What is wrong with me? And now look what that has led to.

Roman's voice came from outside the driver's window.

"Are you okay?" he said. He seemed surprised I was crying. "Is everything okay?"

"Yeah." I swallowed.

"You'll be all right?"

"Yes, I'm fine, don't worry, I'm fine."

"I'll be back in a minute." He wanted to talk to the woman in the kitchen for a few minutes. For some reason I didn't want him to know that he had scared me or that I was upset. I had played a part in front of the camera, and I could play a part now.

It got quiet then. The car was roomy and smelled good, all leather and wood, and I was glad to be alone. I stopped crying. Several minutes went by. I wondered why he was taking so long. Was he talking to that woman? Who was she, anyway? Did she live there? I don't know, but I doubt she asked about me. And I am certain he never told her my name. What was he saying when we were doing it? I don't think he even told me I was pretty.

I sat there for a while in the big fancy car, feeling worried and sad. Finally Roman returned, and we started back down the long road to the gate. As the road swung back down, it seemed terribly dark again. The Valley was ahead of us, but I didn't realize until this moment how secluded we were, concealed from the rest of the world by bamboo and wild brush.

The gravel crunched under the car, and Roman said nothing. I said nothing. What was I supposed to say? *Thanks for the pictures?* I stared out the window. The drive that afternoon from Woodland Hills had, for all his nervous-making questions, seemed kind of cheery. This wasn't. Roman told me he had brought the photographs from the first shoot with him, the ones he had taken up on the hill by Flanco Road. He would show them to Mom and Bob, he said.

"Is there anything you don't want them to see?" he asked.

Was he kidding me? He'd never have the nerve to show them the topless ones, would he? On the one hand, I thought, Well, professionals do what the photographer asks. On the other—this was my *mother*. I didn't want her seeing those. But I was tired of lying. If this modeling job were to go any further, she'd have to find out sooner or later.

It was still a modeling job. Right?

"You can show them all," I said.

Maybe if he showed the topless pictures, I wouldn't *have* to say anything—my mother would get a clue. She'd know something was wrong. Then again, they trusted this man. Maybe if he showed those photos it would just demonstrate that he had nothing to hide. I couldn't figure it out.

But what if he mentioned the asthma? *Oh my God. The asthma.*

For some reason this is what I obsessed about. I would get caught by the lie I had used to try to get away from him. And then I'd have to explain why I lied about having asthma, and then I'd have to tell . . . the Story. Oh God. He was going to ask if I took my medicine, and Mom would say, "For what?"

I felt guilty for lying, as though something I had said had made everything that followed possible. I should have known better.

There was silence, and then, "Don't tell your mother. This will just be our secret."

Roman's voice startled me out of my reverie. His little eyes squinted into the darkness as we drove.

Tell my mother? Is he insane? I'm sitting here inventing

ways to keep my mother from finding out, and he's thinking I would want to tell her.

We turned down sloping Peonia Road, which delivered us almost straight into our driveway at Flanco Road. As we neared I could see the house lights on. Kim was probably there, and Bruce, soon to be my mother's brother-in-law and my uncle. Everyone was probably waiting for me at home, hoping to hear how the camera loved me. This was the moment when a star was born.

The car stopped, and I bolted. My mother opened the door, and I rushed up to her before he could catch up and hissed, "If he asks, tell him I have asthma. I told him that because I didn't want to get in the Jacuzzi." This must have made about as much sense to my mother as it did to me, but I didn't care. I ran to my room, slammed the door, and kicked off my shoes; the avocado shag pile felt good under my feet. I put on my nightgown and sat on my bed in silence. I didn't know what to do. Roman had followed me into the house to see my parents. What would happen? Would he show the topless photos? And if he did, what then? I heard Kim yelling at the dog, and then it sounded like Roman had left. I waited until I thought Roman was gone to call Steve.

As soon as I got him on the phone I started to cry, but refused to tell him what was wrong. I asked him to come over. He probably thought this was my usual drama, that I was just trying to get attention from him since he had broken things off with me. Still, he said he would come. He knew I didn't sound right; he was worried. I waited for him, and when the door opened I expected it to be Steve. But it was Mom. "Why didn't you tell me about the pictures?" she asked. "I don't know," I said.

Gently she closed the door and was gone. She didn't want to make me feel like it was my fault, or I had done something bad. *Maybe this wasn't going be that bad after all*, I thought. She seemed calm. But then, that was my mother, always her calmest when the world was collapsing around her.

When Steve finally arrived, I think I skipped the hellos. "Roman made me have sex with him," I blurted. "He made me do it."

"What? What are you saying? You're making that up!"

Yeah, nothing like a clueless seventeen-year-old boy to confide in. Good choice.

"Roman. He made me do it."

"Do what? He did not."

"Yes he did! After I modeled. I didn't know what to do."

Oh, this was going great. Steve had a stammer when he was nervous—and now, he was very nervous. I was still high, and here was this guy I'd really been crazy about who had been a great friend, and he didn't believe me.

Later, much later, after everything happened, I thought about my friend Ann. She'd gone through something much worse than this and she'd survived. But she'd been unable to say no, too. When she had a chance to just walk with me away from trouble, I couldn't get her to move. This time, I couldn't get *myself* to walk away. I couldn't shout, *Get off me!* or *What are you doing, you moron!*

But, you know, there's something about fame. There just is.

I mean, think about the kids who had sleepovers at Michael Jackson's house and all the accusations that followed. Think about their parents. Were they bad or stupid people? No. They just wanted to believe that being famous made you good.

CHAPTER 5

Much of what happened when I got home was told to me years later; I was too high, and too upset, to remember.

I flew into the house and into my room, but not before my mother got a good look at me. My eyes were glazed and the pupils huge; my hair was damp. *Asthma? Why would Sam say she had asthma?*

Polanski sauntered in, perfectly relaxed and cordial. He must have been a little high himself, but nothing seemed out of the ordinary. After a little small talk, he asked if they wanted to see pictures. They said sure. He went to his car and brought back an envelope of slides, a slide viewer, and a joint. They smoked together.

It's impossible to tell, in retrospect, if Polanski assumed that because of Bob's job at *Marijuana Monthly* we were a permissive family in other ways—more European perhaps? Or maybe he wasn't thinking about it at all. Maybe, with the arrogance of someone who was lauded as a genius around the world, he just assumed that whatever he did was okay.

As Mom and Bob looked at the photos, they were surprised to find them unprofessional, unfocused, cropped haphazardly, with no regard for lighting. Some caught me prematurely, as if the photographer had snapped too soon. My mother knew test shots, and she was instantly baffled why a man of pictures like Roman Polanski would resort to shots like these. I looked more sullen than sultry, one hand on a hip, a hand slightly behind my head, now in my white lace shirt, unbuttoned. No young Marilyn here. When they saw the topless photos, Mom and Bob froze.

"Motherfucker," my sister, Kim, mumbled under her breath. Dogs are pretty good at measuring the mood of a room: Our dog Natasha went into a frenzy, spinning in circles before she peed on the living room rug.

"What are you doing?!" Kim screamed at Natasha, smacking her and dragging her out the door, because she had to do something.

After this, Roman turned to her.

"That's not the way to discipline a dog," he told my sister. Kim looked at him wild-eyed. My mother felt the blood rising into her neck, choking her, her lips stretched thin.

"Get him out of here," Mom rasped.

There was a great flurry of activity. The photographs were shoved hurriedly back into the envelope as Roman explained he had to call someone he was seeing that night. Bob, stunned, handed Roman the end of the roach and practically herded him out the door.

Bob was pacing. "How dare he? Oh my God, that fucker had her take her top off. Should we call someone? Maybe we should call someone." In our house, it was my mother who was in charge. It was her decision.

At first, she tried to soothe herself with the legality of the whole thing. "We didn't sign a release. He can't do anything with those pictures," she said. But it wasn't enough. "He did that with my daughter? He thought that was okay?"

At that point they knew nothing other than that he had taken topless pictures of me—but that, in itself, was enough of a reason for a freak-out. It wasn't just the toplessness alone, though there was that. It was the deception. The betrayal of trust. In their minds *Vogue* meant two things: fashion and clothes. Lots and lots of clothes. The sheer badness of the photos made them realize something was wrong.

Mom and Bob threw out ideas. Call a lawyer. Call Jack. Call Henri and let him know what his friend did. Or, then again: Say nothing. Just keep him away from Sam. They were trying hard to be calm about this, with me in the next room. My mother spoke in a panicked whisper. She went to her bedroom to lie down and think it through. Bob lay next to her and fell asleep. Mom lay there thinking.

Kim came in to check on me. She was at my door, about to come in. She paused. By this time, Steve had come over, let himself into the house, and was in my room. She overheard my conversation with him: *He went down on me . . .*

She turned around, walked to the back of the house, and tapped on Mom's door. Mom was staring at the ceiling, a hand on her forehead.

"He fucked her, Mom," Kim said. Bob woke with a start.

Then, Mom was in my room.

"Did he make you have sex with him?"

I was confused, still frightened, high from the Quaaludes but not understanding it, grateful just to be home, and now my mother had found out. She was quivering with rage. *It's just sex,* I told myself.

"Did that happen? Tell me the truth."

"Yeah," I said.

. . .

That night my mother sat beside me quietly. Occasionally she hugged me and cried a little. I don't remember what she said. Probably nothing. She was lost in thought.

The story that would be repeated in the press for years was that my mother had, for lack of a better term, pimped me out—that she had set me up with Roman as a kind of bait, not only for my career but for hers.

In fact, as improbable as it now sounds, it never, ever crossed her mind that he would have sex with me. First, even though there were movies like *Taxi Driver* and *Manhattan,* which featured a twelve-year-old prostitute and a forty-year-old man's relationship with a high school student, no one talked about real-life child sex abuse. The McMartin nursery school case, for example, where nursery school owners were (falsely and hysterically) accused of ritual sexual assaults on children, was still many years in the future. And however "adult" I may have acted . . . I *looked* like a child.

Then there was Roman's fame. It protected him, but not just in the way people would assume. We wanted something from him—that would be people's first thought. We did want something from him, too. But the idea that my mother looked the other way because of his fame—that's what was false. See, because of his fame, she never for a second thought she would *have* to look the other way. He'd had Sharon Tate. He'd had Nastassja Kinski. Why, if you could have the most scintillating women in the world, would you have a thirteen-year-old girl whose dream date was Steven Tyler and whose best friend was a bird?

But then, the real answer to "Why me?" is quite simple—like Sir Edmund Hillary's answer to "Why climb Mount Everest?"

Because I was there.

Over the years many have said my mother could not have been that naïve; surely she had her own experiences with the casting couch. Well, in fact, she didn't. She was auditioning mostly for commercials, which was a more straightforward business—you had to please a lot of "suits," not artists. She did once have the head of a really big studio call her in because "your head shot has been sitting on my desk and I was intrigued and wanted to meet you." He wanted to know if she had someone to take care of her, and she said, No, she was really fine taking care of herself—and that was that.

But that night, she wasn't sitting and thinking about this rationally. She was thinking what an idiot she'd been. And what she was going to do next. I heard her saying over and over, "The fucker. The fucker. I'll kill him."

After much discussion and back-and-forth, they decided to call Ed. Ed Ehrlich was my mother's accountant. Exactly why she thought her accountant would be the best man to call in a situation like this is a little murky, but it seems that he was, to her, the levelheaded "fixer," the one who could be relied upon to make a cool-headed decision divorced from untoward emotion. And maybe he knew a good lawyer.

"Call the police," he said.

. . .

Within an hour, two cops in full uniform were standing in Kim's room—Kim's, not mine, because mine was in its usual volcanic state. Mom, Kim, and I sat on the edge of the bed. They probably would have sat down if there had been a place to sit, but there wasn't, so they loomed over us. Police often look kind of bored. These did not. The name Roman Polanski had their attention.

"Tell them everything," my mother said.

I never would have been so honest if I hadn't been so high. How I've wished, over the years, I'd never told anyone about that poke in the butt.

I felt like I was on an audition. Only I didn't look at them as they scribbled away. I didn't really speak to them, either.

Why was Mr. Polanski taking pictures of you?

Did he force you to do this?

At any time did he strike you?

Did he offer you alcohol or drugs?

Did he touch you? What did he do? What did you do?

Do you understand what intercourse is?

"Yes," I told the officers.

Did Mr. Polanski insert his penis into your vagina?

"Yes."

Then—did he do anything else?

This took a bit of time. I whispered the answer to Kim. She caught her breath. I think she may have been holding back from crying. She looked at Mom.

"Yes," Kim said to the officers. "He also put it in her butt."

Hearing this, my mother fell back on my bed with her arms out over her head, whispering, "Oh my God." Her reaction really startled me. Was this a terrible thing? Like, worse than the other?

I began the day in homeroom class, and now I was lying on a plastic-covered piece of foam rubber in a curtained-off cubicle in the emergency room at Parkwood Hospital, ten minutes from home. I had been in hospitals before—I'd had chronic bladder infections as a kid—but this time there was a sense of crisis. Police waiting for me in the hallway, two nurses holding clipboards scurrying around silently. And everybody was looking at me—curiously, sympathetically, suspiciously, maybe all three. Nobody talked to me, which was probably just as well since I was sitting there seething.

Being here was my mother's fault. My fucking mother! I wasn't bleeding or bruised. If Mom hadn't called the police, I could be home in my bed now, sleeping it off, instead of here in a drafty green hospital gown after midnight. And they wouldn't let her in the room when they examined me. I wanted her there, so she could see how mad I was.

"Where's my mother? Can she come in?"

"Your mother is right outside, waiting," the nurses said.

"Where's my mother and where's Bob?"

"They're both outside. You'll be able to see them soon."

The doctor came in, and he seemed nice enough, moving through many of the same questions. But I began to get this funny idea that my mother being kept in the waiting area was not the norm and was not an accident. This sense came to me not because the doctor asked me about Mom, but because he didn't. Sooner or later, adults always ask about your mother or father. That's the way it worked. Except with this doctor, and with Roman. They wanted me alone.

"How old are you?" the doctor asked. "I'll explain what I am doing. I won't hurt you." I hadn't thought he would . . . but then again, how would I know? I'd never had a gynecological exam before.

Next thing I know, I had my knees up and out and I was

looking at his face in between my thighs, my feet trapped in those damn stirrups. But my muscles were relaxed—*too* relaxed for someone having an exam like this for the first time. Yet nobody questioned why my body was rubber; if they had, they might have tested for drugs.

The doctor looked inside me, I could feel his fingers through his rubber gloves, not poking but making small circles on the edges before probing deeper, asking me if he was hurting me. He seemed to be looking for something.

"Have you had sex before?"

"Yes."

"How many times?"

Here it was again. The question. I had lied when Roman asked because I thought "once" would sound stupid. I told him twice. If I gave the doctor a different answer, he would find me out somehow, he'd realize I had told Roman one thing and him another, and then I would be the girl who lied.

"Twice," I said. He frowned.

After he was finished and I got dressed, I was delivered back to the hallway and the officers who had come to the house. I stared at my feet. I had this sudden urge to laugh, and then was mortified that I might. What was wrong with me? This was not funny. But the Quaalude was still in my system, and all of the Quaalude looseness and euphoria as well. The doctor returned with more questions and his own clipboard, which he wrote on while nodding kindly. He spoke to the police and to my parents, not me.

At this point, something shifted. It's still hard to say how or why. But we weren't just a distraught family with a kid who'd been raped. If we were accusing some guy down the street, some appalling relative, we might have been more boring, but we'd be believable. In our case, though, we were naming one of the most famous movie directors in the world—and one who, less than ten years after the Tate murders, had a tremendous amount of sympathy in this one-industry town.

"They think we're lying," Mom whispered to Bob.

It was cold in the hospital. In the waiting room, my mother reached for me, but I could barely look at her. I clung instead to Bob. This, too, didn't look good in the eyes of the staff, as I was later to find out.

Eventually, they gave Mom my release papers, and otherwise no definite instructions anyone could recall. Scanning the forms quickly, she caught what she thought was an error.

You have her down as "married," she told the nurse.

"No, ma'am," the nurse said, pointing to the line marked *vaginal condition*. My mother blinked. Vaginal condition: married?

"She's thirteen. She's obviously not married."

The nurse said something about *married* being the word the hospital was encouraged to use to explain my "situation." My mother didn't get it. "But she's thirteen," she insisted. They called for the doctor, who repeated what the nurse had said, and my mother repeated what she had said to the nurse, only louder. The word remained.

You might think that someone might have wondered why I

was such a zombie; a blood test might have revealed the presence of alcohol and Quaaludes. Nobody took my blood. Maybe they just assumed that *of course* I'd been drinking and gulping pills. I was just another screwed-up little skank.

. . .

We left the hospital and drove to the police station in Reseda. I was silent. Bob and Mom were discussing the innuendo they heard in the ER.

We sat in the waiting room. Police stations smell like coffee, sweat, and cigarettes, and everyone here seemed tired. I was moved to a small, cluttered office to sit by myself and wait. It had the standard-issue metal desk and two chairs. The door was closed behind me. On the bulletin board next to me was a report about a man who'd been beaten up and raped with a Coke bottle by two women. I read it twice before the detective came in and introduced himself.

Detective Philip Vannatter was tall and solid and had the face of a high school principal: deep-set eyes, large bushy eyebrows, a permanent expression of furrowed concern. He would later become nationally famous as the chief investigator in the O. J. Simpson murder case. But right now, he was just another smart and tough detective in the Los Angeles Police Department. Unlike everyone else we'd met thus far, he appeared not to have made up his mind about me or the circumstances. He was the first person who didn't treat me like I was lying.

"I'm so sorry you have to go through this," he said.

I let myself smile.

"When did you first meet Mr. Polanski?" he asked.

"About a month ago," I said.

"Did he force you to go with him?"

"No." It would have been hard to explain in an official setting like this how we met, how I wanted to be a model but didn't really want to be photographed by *him*.

"What kind of pictures did he take of you?"

I told him about the photo shoot on the hill, and the shots at Jacqueline Bisset's home, and the shots drinking champagne, and the shots by the lamp at Nicholson's, and the shots in the Jacuzzi.

Did Mr. Polanski give you the champagne? Did he give you drugs? Do you understand what sex is? Did Mr. Polanski have sex with you?

I don't think Detective Vannatter asked me if I had been forced to have sex. This point, I gathered, did not interest him much. He asked the questions calmly and did not rush me. He had a thin, kind smile. This time I wasn't bothered that Mom and Bob had been directed to stay in the waiting area while I had been called away. For the first time all night no one was staring at me curiously, and I felt calm and safe.

I don't recall Detective Vannatter taking notes, but he must have been. He surely had some kind of system, because in the same steady voice he repeated the questions, in the same tone, nodding thoughtfully again, like we were reshooting the scene.

I wasn't undone by the repetition. I didn't think he was trying to trap me. It was clear he just wanted my answers to be accurate. And since I was telling the truth, I felt no pressure to perform.

Still, there was this powerful sense that the train had left the station, and I was on the wrong goddamn train.

. . .

We slept little that night. In the morning, Mom, Bob, and I drove to Santa Monica, a beach town near where we'd lived in Pacific Palisades. We entered the Superior Court of California, a sprawling building rimmed by palm trees. They told me I had to talk to the district attorney. The whole thing had an air of secrecy about it. We didn't even park out front; we had to drive to some underground garage. Maybe there was some perfectly logical reason, but it felt like the whole situation was hush-hush.

Soon we found ourselves in the office of Deputy District Attorney Michael J. Montagna, and staring at drab tiles that reminded me of the floors at school. Tired and just wanting to be cared for, I was acting like a baby. I sat on Mom's lap for a time, then Bob's. I was escorted alone to an office. There were at least two men standing, and a woman sat behind me.

I was seated in a wooden chair across the desk from the district attorney, an older man with dark hair who seemed distinctly unhappy, yet relished his authority over everyone in the room. Everyone else in the room seemed to stay as far away from him as possible.

He looked at me intensely and said he wanted truthful answers. While I had immediately sensed Detective Vannatter believed me, I immediately sensed this man did not. I tensed, partly because of the woman sitting directly behind me. It had been explained to me that because I was female there needed to be a woman in the room, but it made me uneasy that I could not see her but sensed her presence. If she was there to provide me with a sense of comfort, well, it wasn't working out.

At least with Detective Vannatter, it was one-on-one. Our talk seemed private. But here I was surrounded. The other men, whose names I did not know, looked at me deadpan. Even their occasional polite smiles were flat. Again I faced questions about whether I had ever had sex before meeting Mr. Polanski, and other questions about body parts and what Mr. Polanski had done to me and what I had done in response.

Why did you take off your clothes and get into the Jacuzzi?

Where did Mr. Polanski touch you?

Again, did he put it inside you?

Have you ever had sex before? And then: Have you ever had sex with Bob?

With *Bob*?

Now I was furious. I sat rigid with my arms folded, and spit out the answers. I don't think I made a good impression, but then I didn't see why I had to. I was the one who had been raped. Why was everyone asking me about what I'd done with my boyfriend, what I'd done with my *mother's* boyfriend?

I was relieved when it was over, but before I could leave, they had to take my fingerprints. They were investigating the crime scene, and they needed to be able to distinguish all the fingerprints at the home. I was angry—what did I do to be treated this way?—but I was also a kid who'd seen her share of cop shows, so there was something kind of cool about being treated like a criminal. Having seen this kind of thing on TV made it more real.

Throughout the night and morning, I had been asked about Mr. Polanski: What did he say? What did he do? And what sort of relationship did we have?

My mother kept muttering about the son of a bitch who did this to her daughter. But I cannot tell you that over the hours I thought of him even once. I mean, really thought about him. I was not angry at him. I did not feel sorry for him. Nothing. He had quickly become unreal, a man who existed only on paper or film.

Later, though, I wondered: Where was he? What was he thinking? Was he feeling angry with me? Sorry? Was he feeling anything at all?

A day or two later I opened the paper.

There we were.

PART TWO

CHAPTER 6

POLANSKI ARRESTED FOR RAPE

March 12

LOS ANGELES (AP): Film producer Roman Polanski has been arrested and booked on a charge of raping a 13 year old girl. Polanski was arrested Friday night, a day after the rape allegedly occurred at the West Los Angeles home of actor Jack Nicholson. He was released on $2,500 bail.

Police also arrested 26-year-old Anjelica Huston, the daughter of movie director John Huston, on a charge of possessing cocaine. She was booked and released on $1,500 bail.

Police and district attorney investigators took the 43-year-old Polanski into custody at 8 p.m. Friday at the Beverly Wilshire Hotel in Beverly Hills, a police spokesman said.

The complaint against Polanski was reportedly filed by the girl's mother.

Miss Huston was arrested by officers Friday when they went

to Nicholson's home on Mulholland Drive to search for evidence in the rape case.

Police spokesman Lt. Dan Cooke said Polanski and the young girl reportedly were alone in the house at the time of the alleged rape. It was not known immediately where Nicholson was.

Police officials refused to release other details in the case.

Polanski's wife was Sharon Tate. She and four others were murdered in Polanski's Hollywood home by Charles Manson and his followers in 1969 while Polanski was in London.

Roman Polanski was arrested Friday night, March 11, about twenty-four hours after we left Jack Nicholson's. No one called to tell us it had happened. Mom and Bob read it in the newspaper. It was unsettling, thinking that some of what I had told the police officers and Detective Vannatter and the deputy district attorney was now showing up in print for the world to see. That first wire service article said that Polanski had lured a thirteen-year-old girl to Jack Nicholson's house on the pretext of photographing her, then drugged and raped her. He also was suspected of sodomy, child molestation, and furnishing dangerous drugs to a minor.

I'm thinking, This seems like a big pile of Awful for something that took only a few minutes.

Subsequent articles said that my mother and Polanski met to plan the photo shoots, and that my mother was angered after seeing the topless pictures. The implications were obvious: gold digger parents, hot kid as payoff. Several years later, in 1984, Polanski would write an autobiography, *Roman*. He would say that at the time of the first meeting at our house, my mother had asked him to recommend a good agent to her, and that Bob had asked him to pass along an interview request to Jack Nicholson on behalf of his magazine, *Marijuana Monthly*, because Nicholson had been known to support the legalization of soft drugs like pot.

My mother did ask for an agent recommendation. Bob did ask for Polanski to pass along the interview request. Did that imply there was some sort of quid pro quo for professional courtesies that included nookie with the thirteen-year-old? (Neither the agent nor the Nicholson interview came through.)

We also soon learned that during one of the searches of Nicholson's house, Anjelica Huston, Nicholson's longtime girlfriend, had been arrested on charges of cocaine possession. The dark-haired woman at the house who'd knocked on the door during the rape—that was Huston; she wasn't supposed to be in the house that evening, because she and Nicholson had recently broken up. But now I'd gotten her in trouble, too. It might occur to you that making enemies of Jack Nicholson and Anjelica Houston was not a recipe for Hollywood success.

(Incidentally, some of the articles also suggested I had been the one to bring cocaine and Quaaludes to the house. A few pegged me as a drug dealer.)

Later still, we heard more details. After raping me at Nicholson's and dropping me at home, Polanski returned to business as usual. He had a meeting that evening with Robert De Niro to discuss the making of a movie based on a William Goldman novel, *Magic*. (The movie was eventually directed by Richard Attenborough and starred not De Niro but Anthony Hopkins.)

The next day Detective Vannatter and an assistant DA named Jim Grodin went to the Beverly Wilshire Hotel, where Polanski was staying. He was with friends in the lobby, preparing to go out as the two investigators were coming in. They asked to speak with him, and as he separated himself from his group, he asked if whatever they wanted would take more than a few minutes. He was impatient to get on with his night on the town.

He seemed to have absolutely no clue he had done anything wrong—though he did try to inconspicuously drop the Quaalude he happened to be holding; the arresting officer caught him and seized the pill. That fact alone is odd, since Polanski had a prescription for Quaaludes for sleep problems. One can only speculate that maybe at that moment, it seemed too obvious he wasn't using the pills for sleep.

Vannatter and Grodin showed him a search warrant, and once inside his hotel suite they found (but ignored) the little yellow case that held the pills. They also found a photo stub from Sav-On Drugs, where Roman had taken film to be developed. The film included the shots of me in Nicholson's Jacuzzi, naked to the waist.

Lurid tidbits began to leak, slowly but surely, as the press attempted to sensationalize what was already sensational. The Quaalude I'd been given was described as the same drug the actor Freddie Prinze had taken before shooting himself in the head. Anjelica Huston's testimony provided great fodder, too. In exchange for immunity on her cocaine possession charge, she agreed to testify for the prosecution. But her statement seemed to follow the narrative the defense was trying to create. This is how she described me: "[The girl] didn't appear to be distressed . . . she was breathing high in her throat when she came out. She seemed sullen, which I thought was a little rude. . . . She appeared to be kind of one of those little chicks between—could be any age up to 25 . . . you know, she did not look like a little scared thing. . . ." About Polanski himself, she said, "I have seen him as a man with compassion, not someone who would forcibly hurt another person. . . . I don't think he's a bad man. I think he's an unhappy man."

Articles always referred to Roman as the "Polish film director and the widower of murdered actress Sharon Tate." Polanski was not only at the top of his game, he was also something of a tragic figure in Hollywood. There was a subtext to the early articles: Who was this slutty little girl trying to entrap one of the greatest film directors of all time? Hasn't poor Roman suffered enough?

The next two weeks were a blur. Polanski posted bail, and there were TV reports showing him being hustled through crowds of cameras and microphones, with a tall, glowering man with bushy sideburns by his side. This was his lawyer,

Douglas Dalton. The lawyer shook his head vigorously when questions were shouted at him. I began to notice the channel was often changed as I walked into the living room.

When asked why the photographs seemed so amateurish, Polanski explained to friends that they were intentionally blurred, as though taken on the fly. He was inspired, he said, by the British-born photographer David Hamilton, whose dreamy, grainy, often-nude photos of prepubescent girls—ten, eleven years old—were at that time all the rage. While the British newspaper the *Guardian* has noted that Hamilton's photography was "at the forefront of the 'Is it art or pornography?'" debate, that debate was mostly in England and the United States. His work was not at all controversial in France, his home for decades. "It's like the donkey chasing the carrot all his life," Hamilton said of his work in an interview. "Girls girls girls. That's what it's about. Better than playing football or cricket, I guess." That morally ambiguous observation might have just as well come from Polanski himself.

Mom was panicking that my name would appear in the news, a concern that was hardly unfounded. While the American press generally resisted printing the names of rape victims, the European press had a different attitude about such things. There, where Roman Polanski was considered a genius and a cultural hero, I was nothing more than a nuisance and an apostate with no rights.

In his autobiography, Polanski would write how the accusation immediately made him the butt of jokes ("Heard the title of Polanski's next picture? *Close Encounters with the Third Grade*"), and box office poison in the United States. "I was a pariah," he wrote. "'We can't have a rapist in our agency,'" he quoted his former agent Sue Mengers saying. Polanski went on, "Although she later revised this judgment—swung to the other extreme, in fact—her initial attitude was shared by most of Hollywood."

Polanski's memory is faulty here—or maybe just convenient for breast-beating. From the beginning there was little outrage among prominent Hollywood figures. But however persecuted he may have felt here, in Europe there was no debate: he was an extremely sympathetic figure, and it was easier to see him as a victim—if not of a malicious setup, then at least of America's obsession with celebrity and the desire of every aspiring pretty girl to make it, however she could. And Americans—so puritanical, so obsessed with sex and sexual shenanigans!

My mother felt relieved to see him arrested, but I wasn't so sure, still feeling that I had at least in some way brought all this on myself. If I were clever or if I had put up more of a fight, or if I hadn't drunk the champagne or taken the Quaalude or . . . and so on, then I could have figured a way out of Nicholson's house before things got so crazy. Then I wouldn't be in this situation—and neither would Polanski.

I knew I hadn't wanted to have sex with Roman, but did that make it rape? I thought rape had to be violent. When I was told that what he had done was a serious crime because of my age, I was shocked. While I may have been unsure what to call it, I certainly didn't see it as Polanski himself described it later, in his autobiography: "In all my many premonitions of disaster, one thought had never crossed my mind: that I should be sent to prison, my life and career ruined, for making love."

Making love? Really? On what planet could what happened ever be considered "making love"?

Still, I was not brutalized. I was not dragged into the woods. I never felt in physical danger, and I never felt "poor me." At least, not because of being raped.

CHAPTER 7

At the end of March I had to appear before this thing called a grand jury. I didn't know much about it, but I knew I was going to have to tell the details of what had happened at Jack Nicholson's house to twenty-three strangers. This was how the courts determined whether a person could be indicted for a crime, and whether a trial could proceed. Was there enough evidence? Was there *any* evidence? Would I be believed?

I tried not to think about it. I returned to school the week after the rape, and even resumed my acrobatics class, mostly to give the appearance that everything was normal. My name was not yet out, and the news of Polanski's arrest was not a topic of conversation in the average junior high school. Still, I knew it wouldn't be long before people figured it out. I had told my friends about the modeling work I had done with a famous movie director, and my friend Terri, of course, knew I had gone off with Roman that day. People were going to put it together soon and realize that I was The Girl.

I wasn't exactly cut off from the world, but my family made an enormous effort to create a media blackout around me. TVs and radios snapped off, newspapers were hidden; there was lots and lots of shushing.

All that not-thinking-about-it made me nervous. All those concerned, sad eyes pissed me off. I was the surliest everything-is-normal teenager you ever met.

In all honesty, I think I wanted my mother to suffer. Look at the horrible mess she'd gotten us into. If she'd only kept her mouth shut! I didn't look at her, and if I responded to her at all it was in monosyllables. It kills me now to realize what she was going through at the time: overcome with self-reproach, the feeling she'd failed at her greatest responsibility—protecting me. She also had more practical concerns. Those Ourisman Chevrolet commercials that she flew back east every six months to shoot had been the mainstay of our income for years. If she brought bad publicity to the company, if she were no longer their spokesmodel, we could kiss this sunny Valley life goodbye.

No one recalls for sure when my father was notified, though we all assume it was the day after the rape. I think about my dad hearing the news back in York, and his quiet rage is more terrifying than anything my mother's visible fury could produce. I can imagine him crying, too, the way he did when he sent me off at the airport the summer before. They were hot, silent tears, the kind a man cries when he is furious and powerless.

. . .

The morning of grand jury testimony, March 24, 1977, was sunny but unseasonably chilly. Gusts of wind rippled the ocean, which is just a few blocks from the Santa Monica courthouse where the case had been assigned.

We'd driven through a back entrance into a basement garage to avoid reporters, my mother doing her deep-breathing exercises to calm herself while Bob drove. Our arrival was relatively calm. Polanski, on the other hand, had been swarmed outside several days earlier—not only by the press, but by a party of local high school girls visiting the courthouse. They acted like he was David Cassidy, as they shrieked and clamored for his autograph. There was, I heard later, a scuffle between the reporters and the high school girls, each jockeying for position.

The judge overseeing the case was a man named Laurence J. Rittenband. Rittenband never had any doubt about what he would do with his life. He went directly from high school to New York University law school, and then, when he was declared too young to sit for the bar exam, went to Harvard Law School for a few years and graduated summa cum laude. He worked in the U.S. attorney's office in New York City, served in World War II, and eventually moved to California, where he was appointed a judge in Los Angeles Municipal Court, and then to the Superior Court by the governor of California in 1961.

Rittenband was a bachelor and bon vivant, and had an attraction to some of the more provocative figures in jurisprudence. He was reportedly a good friend of Los Angeles lawyer Sidney Korshak, the Chicago mafia's West Coast fixer. At the time of Polanski's indictment, the seventy-one-year-old Rittenband had two long-term girlfriends, according to Polanski film documentarian Marina Zenovich. "I have one that cooks and one that does the other stuff," he boasted. The one who did "the other stuff"—Marlene Roden—was barely twenty years old when she met the judge. Rittenband clearly liked much younger women, and Zenovich hints that he saw a little of himself in Polanski.

The judge took great pride in his membership in the posh and almost exclusively Jewish Hillcrest Country Club. In 1979 the initiation fee was around $50,000 (today, $180,000); members at the time included Groucho Marx, Milton Berle, and Jack Benny. (Danny Thomas was the first non-Jew admitted, causing Benny to quip that if they were going to admit a Gentile, they should at least get someone who looks like a Gentile.) In a town where so much business was conducted on the golf course, membership in this club could make a career.

Personal peccadilloes aside, Rittenband was considered a very smart and fair judge, one who came to trial prepared and would listen to all arguments. At the same time he did not suffer fools. He was not nasty, but he was gruff; he never sugarcoated anything.

He did have one weakness, though, and it turned out to

be a tragic one: he was addicted to high-publicity cases. Over the course of his long career he presided over Elvis Presley's divorce, Marlon Brando's child-custody battle, and a paternity suit against Cary Grant. As the judge with the most seniority in Santa Monica, Rittenband used his power and position to replace the judge originally assigned to the Polanski case. He appointed himself.

Reports of his gossiping about the case with other Hillcrest members were rampant; one member of the club since the 1970s recently told a friend of mine that Rittenband was a "pompous ass" who couldn't resist regaling cronies with details of the cases he presided over. According to a *People* magazine article at the time, the judge, who kept two leather-bound scrapbooks filled with newspaper accounts of his past trials, had scoffed at the notion that Polanski couldn't get a fair trial in Los Angeles. "People here are more sophisticated than anywhere else in the country," he said, "and from what I've been able to gather, public opinion is divided on who is at fault. There are those who think Polanski a devil, and others who wonder why a mother would let her 13 year old daughter go around with a 43 year old film director anyway." The fact that the judge on an active case was sitting for an interview with *People* magazine pretty much said everything about who he was and what he valued.

Anyway, the grand jury was here to see if it could indict Polanski on six counts: furnishing a controlled substance to a minor; committing a lewd or lascivious act; having unlawful sexual intercourse; perversion; sodomy; and rape by use of drugs. I wasn't thinking about this, of course. I was just thinking about sitting under those flat lights, saying what happened, and getting the hell back to class.

In the waiting room, everyone sat dreading their turn and worrying about whoever was in there—Mom, Bob, and Kim. Even Steve had been called to give his version of what I had told him. He might even be questioned about having sex with a minor himself. I had even put the guy I had been so crazy about in jeopardy. He must have been scared to death, only seventeen himself, thinking he would have to recount our one time together. He'd always told me I was too young for him— and now look where he was. His mother was with him and she sat quietly, knitting and occasionally crying. My mother felt sorry that her son had been dragged into all this and she tried to comfort her. But as it turned out, she wasn't crying over her son's involvement in this case. One of her friends was dying of cancer. That didn't make any of us feel better.

My mother was the first witness called. Assistant District Attorney Roger Gunson asked about how she and Polanski had connected through Henri Sera, Kim's then boyfriend, and then about the initial shoot. It's funny, looking back now on some of the things she said. When Polanski presented the idea of this photo shoot of young American girls, my mother said, "I thought he might want younger girls."

Younger! This moment showed how her mind was really working. Somehow she had gotten the impression that he was photographing children. And she didn't think for a second that he was a pedophile. Apparently he had been dating Nastassja Kinski, who was fifteen at the time, but my mother had no idea. His taste for young girls, news to us, would soon be widely publicized. But Kinski, however young, looked like a woman and I did not—and my mother simply did not put me into that category of nubile beauty who would have caught his attention. So it was the idea that I was too old for the shoot, not quite a child anymore, that was worrying her. That Polanski had a sexual interest in her daughter never occurred to her. Truthfully, until that night it had never occurred to me, either.

"Did you ask Polanski if you could go [on the shoot]?" Gunson asked. "Yes," Mom said. "And he said no, that he would rather be alone with her because she will respond more naturally." Mom recounted the story of Polanski's return. "He drew some pictures of pirates for her." I considered myself a decent artist, and I remember looking at Polanski's pirate drawings and not being terribly impressed by his artistic skills. But my mother was thinking of me as a child he was trying to win over with cute little pictures; he might just as well have been sketching ponies and unicorns.

Then they asked about the day, March 10, and my mother almost broke down. "Before she went, she had indicated to me that she didn't like him. . . ." But Mom wasn't answering a direct question, and Gunson asked that it be stricken from the record—because, I guess, it contributed to the idea that she was pimping me out to him in some way. Which, of course, she wasn't. It was just that she had seen in the past how I would blow off things I'd committed to do in this teenage way. She hated that, and she wasn't going to let me do it now. You want a career, kid? Well, suck it up and take care of your responsibilities.

Far from the carelessness she'd been accused of, this nudging me toward Polanski was actually an example of her standing her ground as a parent. You could accuse my mother of cluelessness. But you couldn't accuse her of not wanting the best for me.

Her remark was not stricken from the record.

Then Mom recounted how I had spoken to her from Nicholson's house, and how she asked if I wanted her to pick me up, and I said no—and then how Polanski got on the phone and told her about taking pictures in the Jacuzzi. ("I thought, 'Why a Jacuzzi?' But I didn't say anything. I just didn't.") When I came home, Mom reported, I told her about the asthma. She had no idea why I said this, but tried to cover for me. "[Polanski] asked me about her asthma. . . . And I said, 'Yeah, it's really too bad.' And then he said, 'What kind of medicine does she take for that?' and I said, 'Oh, lots of different kinds,' just fumbling around." When Polanski showed her the photos of me topless from the first photo shoot, Mom tried to take the logical approach. "I decided not to say anything so that Samantha would not feel like she did an awful thing and cause a big scene. I thought I would wait and get him out of the house, because we didn't sign a release for the pictures, and he couldn't print them. And I thought that to be the end of that."

Mom tried to talk dispassionately, but she couldn't hide how weird it all was: me rushing past her, Polanski coming in, showing my family the topless photos from the first photo session, she and Kim being freaked out, the dog peeing on the floor. "It must have been some kind of energy thing happening because she never does that." (It was the 1970s; we talked a lot about strange energies. And dogs really do pick up on things.)

Kim was next. She testified about how she saw the photos, how the dog peed—and how Polanski gave her a big lecture about how she wasn't disciplining her dog correctly. (Dog owners like to be corrected about their discipline techniques about as much as mothers do.) She then talked about how she eavesdropped outside my room while I was talking to Steve.

Then came the criminologist who testified about my panties. To people who are into forensics, this was interesting. He testified that semen was found in the underwear, but not sperm. How? Unclear. Low sperm count, or possibly vasectomy. (But then again, why did Polanski ask me when I'd last had my period if he couldn't get me pregnant? Of course, the test wasn't conclusive. We hadn't seen the last of those panties.) There were also swabs from other parts of my body—vagina, anus—again with the appearance of semen, but no sperm. It was an unfortunate finding for the prosecution; the testing method for semen was known not to be as accurate as the testing method for sperm. First, there was a chance that the chemical used to detect semen was instead detecting enzymes in vaginal fluid; it was all a question of how quickly the chemical applied to the stain changed color. (In this case, it changed color very quickly, indicating semen.) And second, sperm would have helped identify the perpetrator more readily, although not with the almost 100 percent accuracy of today. But at any rate, one could argue (and clearly the defense intended to) that the semen came from someone else.

After the lunch break, it was my turn.

I remember watching a *Twilight Zone* episode like this, where the accused was set off in the shadows, his face alone cast in harsh light. I felt like I was being tried for a crime. Maybe I was. Three rows of middle-aged strangers stared at me stonily as I answered questions. They studied my face, my body, my gestures. I didn't look at anyone. I had this plastic heart-shaped pendant my friend Terri had given me; it was striped, with little rainbow layers of color. I held it tight, and as the questions kept coming at me I twisted it round and round my fingers. No one sat next to me on the stand. Not my mother, not an attorney. In one week I'd turn fourteen. I was put under oath, I was forced to answer every question and told that if I didn't, or if I told anyone what was said in the courtroom, I would be in major, major legal trouble.

This may sound cavalier, but it is true: If I had to choose between reliving the rape or the grand jury testimony, I would choose the rape.

Assistant District Attorney Roger Gunson was a handsome man, in a square-jawed, straight-arrow, Eliot Ness kind of way. He gently placed laminated proof sheets from both shoots in front of me. I didn't really want to look. He started by asking me about that first shoot—how, exactly, did I end up with topless photographs? "Was that at his request or did you volunteer to do that?"

"That was at his request," I replied. It was hideously embarrassing to explain I wasn't wearing a bra because—well, look at me. Did I need a bra?

We moved on to the day in question, step by step by step. Taking pictures at Jacqueline Bisset's house, moving on to Jack Nicholson's, and the various exhibits—what I was wearing.

Exhibit Four: "Does this appear to be the panties you were wearing?"

I looked at them.

"Yes," I said.

It was beyond mortifying. A room of middle-aged strangers thinking about me in those panties. And why did every guy have to call them "panties"? Couldn't they have just said "underwear"?

"After he kissed you, did he say anything?" asked Gunson.

"No."

"Did you say anything?"

"I said, 'No, come on, let's go home.' . . . He said, 'I'll take you home soon.'"

"Then what happened?"

"And then he went down and started performing cuddliness." (My mother didn't want me to use slang when we talked about this. She told me the term was *cunnilingus*. Apparently I didn't quite hear her correctly.)

"What does that mean?"

"It means he went down on me, or he placed his mouth on my vagina . . . he was just like licking and I don't know. I was ready to cry. I was ready to cry. I was kind of—I was going, 'No, Come on. Stop it.' But I was afraid."

It went on like that. I had to talk about having oral sex, having anal sex, being drunk, being dizzy with the Quaalude. They asked me to describe him having an orgasm inside my butt, and the semen leaking out, and the woman knocking on the door, me trying to leave . . . and him guiding me back to the couch. And then, all of it again.

The doctor at the hospital testified that I had not sustained any tears or injuries during intercourse—and that he had not found any semen rectally. Not necessarily because ejaculation hadn't happened, but because—as I'd testified—I'd had a bowel movement after seeing Polanski, thus possibly eliminating the semen. This, of course, is also something every teenager wants to discuss in front of a roomful of adults: pooping.

They asked how often I had had intercourse before. I said twice—which again wasn't true. I had fooled around with my boyfriend; there was kissing, groping. But sexual intercourse had only happened once, with someone I knew well. So why did I hold to this stupid lie? What would the grand jury have thought if they realized I was saying I had *more* sexual experience than I actually did, not less? It's just the kind of thing a dumb kid does, and in this matter, I was a dumb kid—and scared.

The grand jury deliberated for all of twenty-three minutes before returning with the indictment on all six counts. Decades later, in 2009, some of the jurors spoke to the press about that day. One of them was Jean Biegenzahn, who was forty-eight at the time of the grand jury. (I think she was the one person who I actually looked in the eye during my time on the stand. I vividly remember looking up, seeing one woman looking at me sympathetically; then I never looked at the jury again.) Biegenzahn thought I looked like her daughter. "She was so scared, and here are 23 old fogies watching her," she said. Biegenzahn believed me, as did the youngest juror, Joanne Smallwood, then thirty-nine—though she also thought I was "fast" for my age.

There was so much fallout from that day. In his autobiography, Polanski would write that at one of the hearings Gunson's staff saw me and Bob—my mother's long-term boyfriend, a man I considered another father—"locked in a steamy, passionate embrace. It wasn't the avuncular hug of a grown man comforting a young girl—it was more; her leg was between his legs."

I read this now and feel a little queasy. I did, in fact, sometimes regress with Bob; I remember sitting in his lap with my arms around him at one hearing. But the implication of this . . . Did anyone really report that? Did they really believe it?

Polanski and his team acted as if they did. They also knew

no sperm was found. Which must have emboldened them to do what they did next.

POLANSKI PLEADED NOT GUILTY IN DRUG-RAPE CASE

April 18, 1977

(AP) Movie director Roman Polanski pleaded not guilty Friday to a Los Angeles County Grand Jury indictment charging him with drugging and raping a 13-year-old girl March 10 in the home of actor Jack Nicholson. . . .

"I am innocent and can't wait to be vindicated," Polanski told reporters after the brief court session. He was critical of coverage of his case, saying he thought that the news media had handled it "very poorly."

POLANSKI'S ATTORNEY TO SEEK SEX DATA ON GIRL
Los Angeles Times

April 21, 1977

Film director Roman Polanski's attorney said Wednesday he plans to ask for an inquiry into previous sexual activity by the 13-year-old girl Polanski is accused of drugging and raping.

The lawyer, Douglas Dalton, indicated in Santa Monica Superior Court that he will also seek a psychiatric examination of the famed film director's alleged victim.

"The facts that we're aware of," Dalton said, "show that before the events of this case, this girl engaged in sexual activities. We want to know when, where and with whom and why those people were not prosecuted."

. . . Polanski, 43, was asked by reporters how he expected the case to affect his life.

The Polish director, whose wife, actress Sharon Tate, was brutally murdered by members of the Charles Manson family, replied, "I'm used to grief. This is a trifle."

And then, though the transcripts from my grand jury testimony had not yet been released, there was this:

GIRL IN POLANSKI CASE ADMITS SEXUAL AFFAIRS
Defense Files Motions Seeking Dismissal of Six Count Felony Indictment Against Director

May 12, 1977

. . . "I seek to ascertain if she is truthful about her previous episodes of sex," Dalton said in his motion. "It is possible that she fantasizes or lies about previous sexual experiences . . ."

Dalton said the prosecutor, by failing to question her further about when, where and with whom she earlier had sex, in effect deprived the defense of "vital" information that could be used to attack the girl's credibility. . . .

Dalton's motions quoted a statement the boyfriend gave to the district attorney in which the boy said he talked to the girl just after the alleged rape. The girl "is always acting and therefore it was difficult to determine if she was truthful or not," the statement said.

The boyfriend also reported the girl's recounting of the episode was "not in sequence" and she repeatedly said, "I don't believe this is happening to me."

Well, I didn't. But it did.

But here's the funny thing. I remember overhearing adults discussing how fortunate it was that I was not yet even fourteen when I was raped, that Roman was in even more trouble because I was thirteen . . . and I thought, Wait, how is that in any way good? And then, after the grand jury testimony where he was indicted on all counts, I overheard a discussion about how unfortunate it was that there was no physical damage to me—especially rectally. There was this sense of disappointment. If only he'd hurt me worse, in more obvious ways, everything would be better. It seemed very quickly that there was an attitude of winning-and-losing in court, not whether I'd actually been hurt. If the worse I were hurt the better, then why would anyone care that I'd been hurt at all? It is disconcerting to be a young girl and know that people are on your side yet still feel a sense of regret you weren't damaged *enough*.

Almost immediately, from the start of this case, I felt the pressure to be damaged. But I refused to be damaged enough to be a "good" victim.

CHAPTER 8

I t must have been torture for my father to be so far away from the action. I know how upset he was about what happened to me, but also he was an attorney, and I was in legal hell. He was especially outraged that the defense, trying to build a case that I had fantasized the rape, was asking the court to require me to undergo a psychiatric examination. He called his friend Robert P. Kane, the Pennsylvania attorney general, and asked him to recommend someone to handle opposing Polanski's motion. Enter Lawrence Silver.

Larry was a distinguished thirty-two-year-old deputy attorney general of Pennsylvania in 1977 when he quit, withdrew his life savings, put his few belongings in a yellow Porsche, and drove from the grim statehouse of urban Pennsylvania to the sunny beaches of Southern California. He later told me that his plan was to spend a year living by the beach and getting a tan for the first time in his life. It didn't work out that way.

Larry's "year" of mellowing out ended in a matter of weeks

when he was recruited by the business and entertainment law firm Loeb & Loeb. It was a big, prestigious job. They fast-tracked him to a partnership in the high-stakes world of Los Angeles business litigation. Welcome to Hollywood. Thirty-six years later, he's still never gotten that tan.

Kane called him and explained that a friend whose daughter had gotten into a little bit of trouble in California needed a lawyer. Larry said he'd be glad to take the call. My father phoned him moments later.

Dad asked him if he knew about the Roman Polanski case—who didn't?—and told him that the girl who had been raped by Polanski was his daughter, Samantha Gailey. The defense, he explained, claimed Samantha had fantasized the incident, and was demanding that she undergo a psychiatric examination.

Dad was outraged at the California DA for not protecting me, and furious at Polanski's lawyer for an unjustified and prejudicial intrusion. He said that seeking a psychiatric interview of the complainant was not only something he'd never do; he didn't even think the law would allow it. Would he represent me and the family? To his credit, Larry gave him the caveat of his lack of experience in criminal law. But based on Kane's recommendation, Daddy was willing to overlook it. Frankly, I think he thought it was probably a simple matter—one that a civil litigator could certainly handle. Larry told him he'd still have to get clearance from his firm for limited representation. There was some doubt they would allow it; much of their work was in the entertainment business, and he would be going up against a Hollywood luminary. But the prestige of a recommendation from a state attorney general trumped their reluctance. Well, that, and—as I've learned—in Hollywood even the lawyers are celebrity-obsessed. Larry was allowed to take the case.

It was about two weeks after the grand jury testimony that I met Larry, when he came to interview me and my mother. (In my diary I wrote, "Have to meet my new attorney. Bummer.") I'm sure he was gentle and careful with me. But I hated having to go through it all again—asking me about any of the events surrounding the rape, even if he didn't press for details, wasn't the best way to make a good first impression on this girl. I thought I was just sullen, but Larry told me later that the look I gave him when we met was hostile—like *really* hostile. He remembers me seated on one end of our brown sofa in the living room, my face contorting like I'd just bitten into a lemon, then turning away, pretending he wasn't there. He would actually have to direct questions to my mother, who would then ask me. Ridiculous, I know, but I just didn't want to deal with it. I wanted to go back in my room, shut the door, and be alone with my music.

To this day Larry has never asked me the nitty-gritty of what happened in the room at Jack Nicholson's house. I appreciate that, but it wasn't just out of concern for me. As my attorney, it was more important for Larry to know the details of what happened before and after the rape: the meeting with Mom and

Bob, what happened that made Terri, who was supposed to accompany me, not come along. Chronology mattered. Timing mattered. When articles of clothing were removed, when they were put back on (those damn panties again!), who said what, and when. Mostly this information was not essential for my representation; Larry said they were questions that the DA was asking, and he had to have the information. In my mind, I knew that Larry was on my side—after all, my father had hired him—and was just doing his job, but with all his questions, he seemed more like the enemy. I know it wasn't comfortable for him, either, and given the chance, he'd rather have gotten information from Mom, Bob, or even from Kim, who hated talking about it almost as much as I did.

I could see I was trying his patience, but he tried very hard to form a bond with someone who wished he would just vanish in a puff of smoke. He asked about my day-to-day teenage life, dreams, aspirations in that way that adults do to kids, and kids see right through. (He did get points by scoring VIP seats to the Led Zeppelin concert "The Song Remains the Same." He might have been trying too hard, but I knew he was trying.)

Over the years Larry became one of my most trusted allies and true friends, but back then he just seemed part of the hell I was being forced to go through. He was sympathetic, though, and it didn't take long to convince him that my rape was no fantasy. Larry couldn't understand why the defense was asking for the psychiatric evaluation; he said it would only inflame emotions on all sides.

This is not to say the tactic of blaming the victim in a rape case was anything new. Quite the contrary: Even with forensic evidence of sexual activity, the defense tries to manipulate the issue to a he said/she said case, and often attacks the credibility and morality of the victim. Fortunately, two years earlier, California state senator Alan Robbins introduced and passed the Robbins Rape Evidence Law, which prohibited rape defendants from introducing as evidence at trial the sexual histories of their victims. The statute became a national model and was adopted in many states.*

Larry thought Polanski's lawyer, Douglas Dalton, was engaged in legal grandstanding. He was trying the case in the media, starting with the suggestion that of course I must be mentally unbalanced. From the legal point of view, Dalton's strategy was ill-advised because it was a stretch to think the court would order a psychiatric evaluation of me, so he would be starting off with losing his first motion. I know that attorneys fight these battles with each other but still remain respectful of their adversaries. I could see that Larry was starting to dislike Dalton. I started to like Larry a little more.

Larry prepared a draft opposing Dalton's motion, and discussed it with him, hoping to find a compromise of some sort.

---

* In 1981 Robbins stood trial, but was not convicted, for having sex with two sixteen-year-old girls he met in the state capitol in 1978 and 1979. In 1991 he was chucked from the California Senate and served a twenty-month jail sentence for taking bribes from lobbyists. Which proves that even a crooked pol can have a shining legacy.

The basis of his argument was that a witness to a crime was not subject to defense discovery that included a psychiatric examination. They went back and forth without coming to any agreement. Then, before the motion was scheduled to be argued in front of Judge Rittenband, Dalton withdrew it.

We won! Dalton had withdrawn a motion that he had publicly announced he would bring. So . . . Hooray? Well, the truth is, I was so disengaged from what was going on that I wasn't even aware of it. All I knew was that I wasn't going to be dragged to a psychiatrist—a small victory, but a victory nonetheless. I paid no attention to the legal wrangling through this period, and only found out much later through written records, as well as Mom's and Larry's memories.

But at any rate, that was it: Larry's job was done. He dutifully reported the successful withdrawal of the application to my father, who was relieved, grateful, and impressed. Then he said to Larry: "I think this is going to be just the first round, and Samantha and Susan are going to need continuing representation. Would you be interested?" Larry was not by nature a lover of high-profile cases, but he wasn't averse, either. And at this point, he was invested both as an attorney and a human being. Though perhaps he would have had a moment's pause if he realized he was stepping into a modern version of *Jarndyce v. Jarndyce,* the famous case in Dickens's *Bleak House* that goes on for generations. This case he'd just agreed to handle would continue, in one form or another, for the next thirty-six years. (And counting.)

CHAPTER 9

The months leading up to graduation from middle school were kind of a fog for me. My mother, normally a relentless photographer, stopped taking pictures altogether. I think she was afraid that somehow photos from that year could become evidence. Or maybe it was a reaction to seeing the snaps Polanski took of me. We became recluses. Normally Mom loved attention. Now she wanted all of us to be invisible.

My name had been published in Europe,* so now the phone rang incessantly. Mom and Bob changed our number, but soon reporters got the new one. There were some days when all it took was the phone ringing to make everyone jump.

A particularly enterprising photographer in a brown sta-

---

* The U.S. media generally doesn't publish the names of rape victims because of the traditional (and, I hope, outdated) concern that the victims suffer humiliation and harm to their "reputations." Also, one of the reasons that a large number of rapes go unreported is that the victims don't want public exposure. These concerns aren't so strong in Europe.

tion wagon camped outside our house on Peonia Road. I'd peek through the curtains to see the long-range camera lens in the driver's-side window. The presence of that camera changed our movements. We became furtive figures dashing in and out of our own home.

One day a radio DJ from Chicago called, and Bob, in an unthinking moment, actually said my name. Mom screamed at him.

Kim never suffered the intrusions well. One day, when she picked up the phone and someone asked if we were prostitutes, she couldn't stop herself from screaming, "You motherfucker!" Perhaps unsurprisingly, stories started seeping out about this unhinged family at the center of the Polanski scandal.

Rona Barrett, the TV gossip columnist, was one of the few people in the media to provide a measure of decency. She called the house a few times and gently asked if she could sit down with Mom and me, promising that she would not come on strong. By this time my mother and Bob were cynical toward just about everyone's motives, and would hang up on reporters. But this time, Bob picked up the phone, and something in Barrett's voice practically broke him.

"Please," Bob said. "Don't do this. We're having such a rough time. Please help us protect her."

"It's okay, I understand."

Dozens of reporters had said that, only to call again, or show up at our doorstep. But Barrett was true to her word and never called again.

My family really, really needed to get away. With my mother looking for serenity, we took a mini-vacation in Miami with my mom's sister Kathy and her boyfriend, Bruce, to attend a "Holi," a Hindu festival of spring. At the airport I was scolded for having a notebook I'd covered with the brilliant observations of 1970s teenagedom: "Life's a Bitch and Then You Die," "Sneer at Death Fear Only Loss of Pride—Aerosmith." Mom was always worried someone might get a photo of me that made me look bad, and I was angry and tired of being told how to act.

What I remember of the Holi was running and dancing and being sprayed with colored rose water in a park. But that wasn't the main point. Kathy and Bruce were followers of Guru Maharaj Ji (now known as Prem Pal Singh Rawat), who preached that an individual's need for fulfillment can be satisfied by turning within to connect with a constant source of peace and joy. Here's a taste of him:

> *This universe is amazing, but the fascinating thing is not understanding this universe, but understanding that what powers the universe happens to be within us right now, and we can experience it. And when you do, you are filled with peace, with clarity, with joy.*
>
> *This is when you experience the truest, truest happiness.*

Call them cults, or call them personal growth movements: Today people tend to forget how many intelligent, well-educated people were experimenting with them at the time. My mother, for example, consumed therapies like potato chips—Gestalt, Fritz Perls, J. Krishnamurti; she loved the idea of change, of growth. (On the other hand, my father Jack once said to her, "I don't want to grow. I'm grown. I like myself the way I am"—which was probably the beginning of the end of their marriage.) She also spent a weekend at the Esalen Institute in Big Sur, California. Popularized as an iconic weekend of free love in the 1969 film *Bob & Carol & Ted & Alice* and preaching "the continual exploration of human potential," the Esalen movement counted among its followers Buckminster Fuller and Linus Pauling. It was *good* to be a seeker of truth, and if the truth was found by listening to some guy who was, say, an itinerant banjo player before deciding he was God, well, so be it. (That would be Mel Lyman, who founded the Fort Hill Community, a transcendentalist hippie commune based in Boston that more or less declared him a messiah and his music sacred. It attracted a number of wealthy and influential followers until the desire to rob banks began to take precedence over seeking world peace.)

Whatever you may think of it, at a time of chaos in our personal lives, Guru Maharaj Ji gave my family comfort. And while at fourteen I was by no means attuned to his teachings, just being in this environment gave me a sense that you could transform the bad things in your life into a chance to learn—and transcend the badness.

After the Holi we came back to Woodland Hills and I celebrated my birthday with family and a few friends—Steven, Terri, and a new boy who was vying for my attention and helping me get over Steve. But it was a subdued occasion, with my mom trotting out the giant carrot cake, complete with orange-frosting carrot on top, that made its appearance on all festive family occasions.

For Easter break, I flew back to York, Pennsylvania—a glorious break, really. Everyone assumed that the night with Polanski was an event that would make me shy away from sex for years. That's what people expected, and seemed to want. The contrarian in me rebelled. I met and befriended John, the boy (almost literally) next door, a cute, shaggy Shaun Cassidy–like strawberry blond who seemed to adore me as soon as we met. After the last awful month, which included not only Roman but also being dumped by the first boy I cared about, this is what I needed. An evening of making out on the porch on April 1 led to a gift—a cross on a chain—the next day, which led to drinking, getting stoned, and wonderful sex—a first—that night. There is something so earnest and yet sexy about getting a cross as a present.

I was barely fourteen, and I suppose I should have felt guilty. I didn't. I felt I deserved to wash away the bad experience with a good one, and John was the equivalent of a long, hot shower. My father was furious when he found my friend's rolling papers at my house, but he softened on my last day there. We all came over to my house and watched George Carlin on television. I left the next day to face all the problems at home. But at least I was feeling hopeful about the summer.

As difficult as it was to head home and face more of Roman's denials, and more vilification of me and my family, it was nevertheless my best year in school. My drama club teacher, Mr. Mallot, was my favorite: he really liked me, and even though I was no one's idea of a rising star—I tended to get the roles of stenographers and chorus girls—drama felt like a safe, comfortable place to be. (Which seems to be some sort of eternal verity for school outcasts, as anyone who lives for *Glee* can confirm.)

Other teachers were also, shall we say, alternative. One of my teachers filled her thermos with so much booze we could smell it across the room, and at least one of the teachers dealt pot to supplement his dismal high school income. (In the late 1970s, pot was quite a different drug than it is today: much weaker, sort of like a hefty glass of wine that would give you a gentle rainbows-and-sunflowers high, as compared to today's considerably more powerful hallucinogen.)

In fact, even the teacher/student relationship was wildly different than it is today. Our relationships with teachers were warmer and fuzzier—and yes, as we got older, they sometimes crossed the line. But even when there were instances of creepiness, there was generally not a sense of criminality. In fact, not just teacher/student, but any relationship where there was an obvious power imbalance—as with myself and Polanski—well, those kind of relationships were not as frowned upon then as they are today.

I had reason to think about this recently while reading about the case of widespread sexual abuse in the 1970s and

1980s between teachers and students at Horace Mann, an elite New York City private school. One revered teacher, a professor of English as well as a chaplain and cross-country coach, who was accused of having sex with numerous boys, is now eighty-nine and lives in Santa Cruz, California. He explained his behavior to the *New York Times.* "The only thing I can assure you of was that everything I did was in warmth and affection and not a power play," he said. "I may have crossed societal boundaries. If I did, I am sorry."

It's interesting, his choice of words. If you're the wrong age—too young, too old—you would read this and think, What a load of self-justifying horseshit. But if you hit that sweet spot—if you were anywhere from thirteen to forty-five in the 1970s—you could understand he really meant it, believed it, and even lived it without calculation or malice. There was something considered generally positive about erotic experience then, even in the absence of anything beyond the sex itself. The idea was that emotional growth came about through an expanded sexuality—for both the person in power *and* the relatively powerless. This is important to consider, because this is the cultural paradigm Roman Polanski was sopping up in 1977. As wrong as he was to do what he did, I know beyond a doubt that he didn't look at me as one of his victims. Not everyone will understand this, but I never thought he wanted to hurt me; he wanted me to enjoy it. He was arrogant and horny. But I feel certain he was not looking to take pleasure in my pain.

But I was in pain. I still remember an afternoon soon after

the rape, when I was feeling . . . I guess I would say "bottled up."
I took out a razor blade, and started making teeny, tiny cuts on
the inside of my wrist. Not enough to do any real damage, just
enough to hurt. Those pinpoints of blood made me feel better.
They also gave me an excuse to get attention from Steve, whom
I still wanted. I made him swear not to tell his mother, which of
course he did, which prompted a call to *my* mother, and it was
completely embarrassing because I had no intention of kill-
ing myself. But looking back, using that physical pain to dull
my emotional pain was exactly what I was doing. I understand
"cutting"—and I can comprehend why girls do it.

CHAPTER 10

As spring gave way to summer, Larry got a call from Roger Gunson advising him that certain news organizations had petitioned Judge Rittenband to release the grand jury testimony, and that the district attorney would not oppose that request. He didn't expect that Defense Attorney Dalton would oppose it, either, and heard that Rittenband had already decided to grant the motion to release the transcripts of the grand jury testimony.

The grand jury testimony they were particularly interested in was mine, my mother's, and my sister Kim's. It discussed the events of that evening in graphic detail, events that thus far had not reached the public eye or the eyes of any of my friends, classmates, or teachers. It seemed that all the parties had an interest in trying this case in the court of public opinion. All the parties but me.

The judge and the district attorney's office were touched by politics, and there was a benefit to them in being cooperative and cozy with the media. They, and particularly Judge Ritten-band, were not immune to enjoy being the center of attention, and the release of the transcripts would only heighten anticipation and awareness of the upcoming trial. The defense would get the damaging allegations out earlier and could start trying the case in the media, campaigning to destroy my credibility by innuendo and lies without being challenged by the rules of legal practice. The most damaging portion of the grand jury testimony was that it would identify me by name and provide public access to my home address. The release of that information would be a disaster for my family's privacy, and it wouldn't exactly work wonders for my mental state either. Nobody likes the sense that people are whispering about them behind their back, the sense—or the certainty—in my case that I'd arrive somewhere and everyone would say, "That's the one. You know what happened to *her?*" Teenagers are self-conscious for no reason whatsoever. Imagine having one really, really big reason. I had never felt so hideously singled out—and so alone.

It was clear we had to do everything we could to oppose the release of the grand jury testimony. DA Roger Gunson told Larry it would be an uphill battle because of Rittenband's coziness with the press.

It seems shocking now, but in 1977 there was no precedent in California—or in any of the fifty states—for protecting the privacy of a victim who had testified before a grand jury. Larry did research, research, and more research and could find no such case. Nothing. This was a huge problem. It seemed so obvious to us that the transcripts shouldn't be released, but astonishingly the law wasn't on our side. It's not like Larry could go before the court and argue, "Your Honor, trust me—I know I'm right." Unable to find a legal precedent, Larry looked for an analogy—a much weaker authority, but at least something to take to the court. His question/argument became: "If the state of California doesn't do anything to protect the identity of victims, what efforts do they ever make to protect the identity of anyone?" This was not just "out-of-the-box" thinking; it was *miles away* from the box.

What my clever attorney found turned yet another concept on its ear. California protects juvenile crime *perpetrators'* identities from public disclosure. The theory (a good one, I believe) is that if we label a juvenile as a criminal publicly, the chances of his reformation or rehabilitation are substantially reduced, so by protecting that privacy, both the youthful offender and society may benefit.

It was a little far-fetched, so Larry thought the argument might be more moving if he presented it orally rather than putting it before the court in writing. We knew that Judge Rittenband had already made his decision before Larry had even entered the courtroom. We had this one chance—a long shot—to change his mind. Larry was confident in our position but uncertain about the outcome. Judge Rittenband was sensitive to public opinion, so Larry's message was going to be "If you rule against my thirteen-year-old client, people may think less of you."

As Judge Rittenband started to announce his decision, Larry interrupted and said, "May it please the court, I represent the victim in this case and I would like to address the court on the issue of the release of the grand jury testimony." He then made a detailed argument that there were statutes that protected criminal perpetrators from public disclosure, including testimony or reports about their criminal behavior. He provided citations. He argued that had the victim in this case been the accused criminal, the policy of the state of California would be to protect her privacy and not to permit disclosure of her name and identity.

"Is it the policy of the state of California," Larry argued, "that we would provide greater protection of privacy to a juvenile criminal as compared to a juvenile victim? Does it make any sense for this court to release the name of a juvenile victim when this court would be precluded by the policy of the state of California and its statutes from releasing the name of a juvenile charged with the same crime?"

Judge Rittenband sat motionless for what seemed like an hour to Larry, but was probably only a couple of minutes. Then he spoke. "It is the policy of this state to protect the identity of criminal perpetrators if they are juveniles. It would make no sense to release the identity of a child who was a victim. Consequently, the motion for the release of the grand jury testimony is denied, and it will not be released pending further order of the court."

It would be nice to think the judge was persuaded by the

morality of Larry's points, but I believe he was measuring the public reaction and possible criticism for "outing" me. It didn't really matter. I was happy, and my identity would continue to be protected. For the moment.

· · ·

In that awful spring leading up to ninth grade graduation, I was intent on getting a boyfriend—and I got one. Sort of. Ron was one of the wilder boys in school; he was a partier who rode dirt bikes and hunted rattlesnakes in the hills. I was a little afraid of him, which made him all the more alluring. And even though Ron and I didn't last very long—there were a few weeks of endless kissing and getting caught by Nana before I got scared and called it quits—we are friends to this day. (He is, in fact, my children's godfather.)

The pressure from the press continued to heat up. Despite the best efforts of everyone around me, most grown-ups in my neighborhood eventually learned that I was The Girl in the Polanski case. (The newspapers had identified a girl in Woodland Hills, and before March 10 I'd told a few people I was modeling for Roman Polanski. It wasn't hard to fit the pieces of the puzzle together.) Kids weren't really paying attention—but then a camera crew showed up at school. You know that recurring dream we all have where we forget to put on our clothes, and go out in public naked? This felt like walking around school naked.

Adults were often more judgmental than kids. I remember

the day things went south between me and my friend Terri. It was toward the end of ninth grade and, as was often the case, she and I were hanging around my house. My uncle Bruce, an amateur photographer, was showing some of the footage he'd taken of the Holi with his guru, Maharaj Ji. At some point, Terri's very conservative Catholic father showed up in our driveway—just in time to see a houseful of hippies heading out to their cars. He smelled incense and thought it was pot. He and my mother argued loudly. He said something about me being a slut and that Terri couldn't come to my house anymore. He took Terri by the arm and put her in the car. I was furious with my mom for fighting with him, and she was furious that he—a neighbor—was acting this way.

There is a certain kind of religious mind-set that believes girls who get raped deserve it. If you were morally sound, God would protect you from rape. And therefore, you must be as guilty to have been a rape victim as the rapist was to rape you. No one quite articulates it that way, but that's the way many people really think.

Terri went to another school for tenth grade. We tried to stay in touch, but that was pretty much the end of our friendship. I was devastated. I knew she wouldn't argue with her father. I tried to pretend I wasn't hurt, yet I felt utterly betrayed. It was one thing for me to be branded as a slut by an anonymous tabloid, but quite another when it came from the father of a close friend, someone who knew me. Someone who should have known better.

But if there were some very hard times during the months leading up to my graduation from ninth grade, I have to say this: I was saved by the decency and loyalty of the kids closest to me. I remember one evening in particular with a couple of friends, including a boy named Scott. Scott was a year younger than I was, kind and handsome and very indulgent. We'd practice the dances of the day together—the hustle was our particular fave—because his mother had a dance studio. And he would watch *Bugsy Malone*—my movie obsession at the time, a British musical gangster film acted entirely by kids—over and over with me, and let me act out all the parts. (When we reconnected as adults, I wasn't surprised he was gay, but at the time I just thought he was the best friend ever.) In any case, one day a few weeks after my rape, he and another friend were over at my house discussing the details of the case, which was all over the news; they were riffing in the way only preteen boys can. This was right before my identity in the neighborhood became common knowledge. The media had been going on about Mom—what a relentless stage mother she must have been, to pimp out her daughter to a known wild man—and the boys were talking about how disgusting this mother must be. Of course, they had no idea they were talking about *my* mother. "I'd love to meet the mother of that girl and tell her what an ass she is," Scott said.

I couldn't take it anymore.

"You *have* met her," I said. And then I told them the story.

Maybe it was because they were stand-up guys, or maybe it

was because they simply couldn't wrap their minds around it, but Scott never told a soul until 2009, when Polanski was arrested at the Zurich airport and I told him it was fine to talk. That kind of discretion is unusual in anybody, never mind a thirteen-year-old boy.

The media's interest continued to intrude in all aspects of my life, but I think it was the school incidents that made me feel the most vulnerable. Like the day a creepy photographer/reporter caught me outside my last-period drama class and began firing questions at me before I realized who he was and what he was doing. He was stalking me for photos he could sell to tabloids (later the photographs appeared in a German magazine). I'd put the incident behind me until someone told me that the local paper—the *Valley News*—was going to publish one of the photos the next day identifying me as The Girl in the Polanski case.

I was panicked. It was the one time in those early days that I called Larry. He was out of the office, but I told them it was an emergency, that they had to track him down and get right back to me. This was before cell phones, but they paged him. He got the message while driving down Olympic Boulevard. He pulled over and called me from a pay phone on the street outside a carwash. It was a sweltering hot day and the sun beat down on him in his heavy suit and tie.

Newspapers at that time did not publish the name of rape victims, let alone underage rape victims. The threatened publication cast doubt on whether I *was* a credible rape victim, or an ambitious young girl victimizing this famous director to cash in.

With the sun beating down on his head, and cars whizzing by on the street, Larry immediately called the newspaper. There was no point talking to an editor with a scoop; that was like shooing a vulture away from a carcass. So he asked for their lawyer. He told him what the issue was, and said that in the event that this photograph was published, it would constitute an invasion of my privacy. The lawyer argued (that's what lawyers do) that I was in the public eye. I wasn't. Not then. And wouldn't be unless they put me there. The public didn't know who I was. They argued about the basis for Larry's demand, which also included the (arguably) moral obligation of a newspaper to not cause harm with their reporting. It's funny to think of Larry having this heavy philosophical argument from a pay phone outside a car wash.

Their lawyer told him that stringers—people not in the employ of the paper—had secured what they believed, but were not absolutely certain, was my photograph, taken while at school, suggesting that since they were not employees of the paper, the paper was not liable. Larry countered: "Won't you be embarrassed or even economically liable if your paper publishes the wrong photograph or identifies the wrong person?" He added that this trespass on the school property to secure an unconsented-to photograph of a student was likely to be a crime, and that the publication by the *Valley News* would then be aiding and abetting a crime after the fact by paying people to have committed a criminal act. Larry did not back down. He knew what was at stake for me.

The paper's attorney was noncommittal. My mother and I were frantic waiting for the paper to come out the next day.

They did not publish the picture.

CHAPTER 11

In the summer of 1977, America became a little bit unhinged. Fuel prices were so high and shortages so common that citizens band radio, or CB, culture took over, started by cross-country truckers intent on circumventing police surveillance. *Smokey and the Bandit* was a huge hit. It was also the summer of *Star Wars* and *The Deep* (and thus the time when Jacqueline Bisset, who'd offered me wine at her house, truly became an American superstar). Jimmy Carter was the new president.

Elvis Presley died; Apple computers were born. And in what might be regarded as the birth of the gay rights movement in California, two hundred thousand protesters marched through the streets of San Francisco to protest Anita Bryant's anti-gay remarks and the murder of Robert Hillsborough, the gardener attacked and killed by four men screaming "Faggot."

While I was an unwilling part of the news of the day, I was oblivious to the larger currents of social change. After graduating from middle school, I moved back to York to be with my father for the summer. I met his new girlfriend (and eventual wife), Jan, who was a lovely, down-to-earth, fifties throwback of a woman, very Betty Crocker, as different from my mother as it's possible to be. She was wonderful to me, and I was a bitch. I hope that everyone who was like me at fourteen will stop what they're doing for a minute, put down this book, and send flowers and an apology to the good stepparent who put up with them.

For me, the summer was an escape from all that was going on with Polanski back in California. I look at my diary from the time, and it reads something like this: *blah blah blah boy blah blah blah pot blah blah cute boy blah blah liquor cabinet.* These entries, of course, were preceded by this thoughtful observation several months earlier: *I got my pics taken by Roman Polanski and he raped me, fuck.*

I was intent on restoring normalcy, and to me that meant hanging out with my friends, listening to music, getting high, and making out with boys. My partner in crime was my BFF (as they'd say today), Michele, whom I'd been tight with since elementary school. Michele was having a very hard time herself that summer. A male relative, an awful, scary guy, was getting drunk at nights and being abusive toward her. She was afraid to tell her mother. And so it continued. Several months earlier, she had seriously considered hurting herself. As it happened, it was the night I was with Polanski. For years we convinced ourselves that these two awful things happened on the same night because we had some sort of psychic bond: I was hurt, so she had to hurt herself. Nothing beats a teenage girl's capacity for self-dramatization.

But at the same time, our dramas were real, and our desire to escape them was also real. We hung around in a little gang that summer: me, Michele, and a group of boys who could ping-pong back and forth between being our pals and our love interests in a matter of hours. Our parents were at work, and none of us went to camp. (My one-week experiment with camp ended when I begged, and was permitted, to come home. I hated the girly-girls, hated making lanyards, and the only thing I remember enjoying there was liberating the poor box turtle a bunch of kids had caught and stuck in a cage—my final defiance against the system.) Mostly we hung out in the parks, playing ball and getting high; the kid who scored some beer or weed was always the most popular. Getting in trouble was our hobby. Nothing major (I saved that for the next summer), but we worked on creating just enough mayhem to piss people off. I don't think any of us acted out because we were "damaged" by our traumas; we were just young teenagers on the prowl. When we went anywhere we always walked four or five abreast in the street, never on the sidewalk. Not that we were looking to annoy people, though there was that; mostly it was because we didn't want to have any of us have to walk behind the other and be left out of the conversation. We were pack animals.

When we got boyfriends, there was endless scheming over how and when we would see them. When we didn't have boyfriends, we were on the prowl. Everywhere we went—Hershey

Park, out for dinner with my dad, the local ice show—we were scanning the place for boys. (A word of advice to today's teenagers: Ice Capades is generally not the best place to meet boys . . . unless you are a boy.) Innocent moments could turn sexual in a heartbeat. One moment we were swimming with a neighborhood boy named Tom. The next moment he'd pulled out his penis and was proudly showing it to me. I don't remember why. I probably asked to see it. At that point, you didn't really need much pretext for events like that.

John continued to play the part of my main squeeze. My only goals in life at that point were to listen to Aerosmith, stay a little bit numb at all times, and make out with John. We had a poolroom in our house and a stereo system, an ideal gathering place for our gang. (However, for some reason, it was where my father stored his collection of antique glassware—how excited would he be about a bunch of teenagers playing eight-ball around his Lalique?)

My jazz-loving father (his sound track was Miles and Coltrane) noticed that his daughter was going off the rails, so he began instituting rules about how and when I saw John. No kissing on the front porch—and absolutely *no* being alone in a room together. For this reason, I think we managed to have sex once, maybe twice the whole summer. I was furious.

I think my heightened interest in sex *was* a reaction to the rape. My reasoning went like this: If I had had to put up with a creepy old man taking what he wanted from me, why couldn't I give freely what I had to give to someone I loved? *My* body, I thought. *Mine.* Of course, I was about as likely to have a mature relationship with someone as I was to win an Oscar. Sex at that age wasn't about connecting with another human being; it wasn't even about orgasms (at least not for the girls—all the manuals were telling us it was our right to have them, but try telling that to a fourteen-year-old boy). And if you had sex once or twice, it wasn't something you necessarily continued to have. It was more like this toll you paid to cross the bridge to adulthood.

Nevertheless, I was determined to control my own life, and having sex was an important part of this control. There were the usual buckets of teenage rebellion, of course. But there was something else. I realize that many women who've been raped take a long time before they want to be touched again. My attitude was different. I think I wanted to replace a dark, chaotic experience with something pleasurable and normal— and within my control. John was the "man"—or boy—for the job: we were as in love as you could be at fourteen or fifteen, and he made me feel adored and desired and good enough. And oh, how I needed that.

Sure, there were times when I thought of what happened, times when it snuck into my consciousness. But I didn't want to remember. I didn't want to be damaged.

And here's the thing: Back then, I didn't think I was. Not by the rape, anyway. It seemed the entire world was telling me I was either his little slut or his pathetic victim. I was neither. Why did everyone want me to be one or the other?

Of course, within that wistful hope for normalcy there was a great deal of denial and dopey behavior. Before I ever became sexually active my mother had taken me aside and given me some sort of spermicidal cream, which I used the one time I had sex with Steve in California. So I was cautious and sensible enough there, even at thirteen. But then there was Polanski, and then York, and I didn't bring protection with me. (And if you think in 1977 the average fourteen-year-old boy was thinking of using a condom . . . please.) So it was perhaps a blessing my father at least put obstacles in my path. Things could have been a lot worse.

But that summer all I remember is the sense of relief that I was not in the thick of it. I had this vague sense of a storm gathering back in California without me. I wrote in my diary: "If the publicity gets too bad maybe I could stay here. Maybe they won't be able to find me."

. . .

I wasn't wrong about the "gathering storm." While I was being a brat in York, all the parties were getting ready for Polanski's trial in Southern California. Despite the overwhelming evidence, it was impossible at that point to know which way a trial would go. On the one hand, the defense had done a really good job rallying support from the Hollywood community, spreading lies, and using the press to discredit me. On the other, Polanski had many of his own impending troubles. Shortly into the proceedings in mid-April, Polanski, with the judge's consent, had retreated to his home in London to escape the press (I wonder if a noncelebrity would be given this professional courtesy). Unbeknownst to us at the time—and something that would have undoubtedly come out at trial—the magazine that Polanski was allegedly doing the photo shoot for, *Vogue Hommes* (not *Vogue Paris* as we had always believed), was essentially saying to him: Photo shoot? What photo shoot?

In Polanski's version, recorded in his autobiography:

*When I tried to call [*Vogue Hommes *editor Gerald] Azaria— the same Azaria who had begged me for an interview and urged me to undertake the layout that had led to my troubles—he refused to come to the phone. I went to see [*Vogue *publisher] Robert Caille and explained how essential it was for Azaria to testify that I'd been working on a bona fide assignment. After hemming and hawing, Caille finally said, "He can't do that. You had no formal, written agreement." I certainly didn't, but then, I hadn't even had one for the *Vogue *Christmas issue until it was almost on the newsstands. I said everyone in *Vogue *knew I'd been offered the assignment.*

"Look," said Caille, "we've already been questioned by a man from Interpol. He came to ask about your assignment. We said we knew nothing about it."

I felt betrayed.

By the time Polanski published this, Caille had died, so we may never know what really happened. It's entirely possibly he did have an assignment, and the editor at *Vogues Hommes* was too afraid to stand by it, for fear of being connected to the scandal. But it's safe to say that the inability to produce any real assignment wouldn't look good to an American jury.

Meanwhile, there were the many hearings. Whenever there was a court date where Polanski was expected to show up, news organizations placed a full camera crew with reporters at each door. There were five entrances; that meant that every television station had to employ five full camera crews for the three-second Polanski sighting. I heard that the halls of the courthouse, usually a ghost town, were packed body to body. To get in and out under the radar, my usually impeccably dressed attorney, Larry, would wear running clothes, sweatpants, and a pullover sweatshirt. If you're not in a suit you're not an attorney, so in the sweats he wouldn't be stopped by the press and legal groupies.

Although a date was never definitively set, it seemed a trial was inevitable. There was a kind of ticking-clock feel to it all. And at that point Judge Rittenband did something truly odd— and something only the presiding judge in a courthouse could do. He ordered that the courtroom next to him be emptied, the tables and chairs ripped out. Then he ordered rows of tables and phone lines installed in order to accommodate local, national, and international reporting of the trial. Thoughtful to the needs of the press, to be sure—but perhaps a little *too* thoughtful? Not to mention expensive to taxpayers. This was the age before the twenty-four-hour news cycle, before TruTV, before the notion of court as theater. (Though it was the beginning of it all . . . there was a group of retirees known as the Santa Monica Court Watchers: smart people with time on their hands whose hobby was following court cases. Judges and attorneys used to welcome them in the courtroom, and go out to dinner with them to explain the cases.)

With all the talk of Polanski's lawyers forcing me to undergo psychiatric examination to see if I was fantasizing the rape, lawyer Larry decided to make a preemptive strike: he'd find his own psychiatrist to examine me. He didn't do this to puncture my credibility, as the defense wanted to do, but rather to provide me with support, and comment on the effect of going to trial. Naturally I didn't see it this way. To me this was another invasive adult demanding that I explain myself. You want to see obstinacy? Drag a fourteen-year-old girl to a shrink against her will. It felt like I was being punished for getting raped.

I did end up answering questions, though. The person was nice, asked regular questions, and even I couldn't stay bitchy enough not to answer. Before I knew it, it was over. The psychiatrist found that I was a healthy teenager but said there was no way to predict the wilting effects from the trauma of being cross-examined in open court. This was before the age of cameras in the courtroom, but given the laser focus that would fall on me, I would, in effect, be testifying in front of an international audience reaching millions. Larry knew that any person, let alone a fourteen-year-old, would be stretched to the limit by an ordeal like that. The rape, at least, had occurred in private. This would be public.

. . .

While I was the costar of the Rape Scandal that went on in the press, I was only a bit player in everything that went on during the pretrial posturing. One of the more grotesque scenes was the dramatic "Splitting of the Panties." (Actually, my sister's panties, borrowed without asking.) I didn't know any of the details until years later. This is what Larry told me:

"When you were examined by the police, they took your rust-colored underwear as evidence. During the grand jury, the state's forensic expert testified that the underwear had been tested, and that seminal fluid, but not sperm, was evident—a curious finding, but not unheard-of. Now, both sides wanted to test the underwear for the presence of sperm before the trial—and both sides were laying claim to the panties. Judge Rittenband's Solomonic solution was to cut the panties in half, so both sides could take samples to their individual labs.

"The question was: How and where to cut? The stain on the panties was not regular in shape, more like a gerrymandered congressional district. The problem was compounded by the fact that the density of the stain was also not easily divisible; it seemed to be two stains, and two compounds, overlapping each other.

"So imagine—seven men, including a representative from

the medical examiner's office, Douglas Dalton, Roger Gunson, and me, staring down at your underwear—in a basement room of the courthouse.

"We argued for over an hour whether to cut the stain this way or that way, with various suggestions proffered. I wanted four sides snipped, with each side getting samples from both parts of the stain, but I was shot down. Dalton and the medical examiner's man argued strenuously, drawing lines in the air with a pointer. Finally, a technician wearing latex gloves gingerly began cutting, zigging a bit this way, zagging a bit the other way, as he if were cutting out letters for a science fair poster board.

"Finally the deed was done, the panties snipped, with the prosecutor's sample going to the Los Angeles County medical examiner and the defense's sample, courtesy of Dalton, going to a medical lab of their choosing in Arizona."

Why were these panties so important? Well, at this point everything was important, and evidence gleaned by the panties might determine whether there would be a trial, which everybody seemed to want. The judge wanted to sit on top of the inevitable international media frenzy. The DA's office wanted to prosecute the criminal and put him away. The defense felt emboldened because of the public success of their campaign to destroy my credibility and was confident it could be extended to the courtroom. The press wanted the trial for the same reason that sharks like swimming around popular beaches. The only ones who *didn't* want a trial were me and my family. My parents believed it was more important to protect me than to see Polanski get a long sentence.

The only way out was a "plea bargain." Polanski would plead guilty to some lesser charge, get a judicial slap on the wrist, and we could all leave the whole sordid mess behind. If the facts gleaned from examining my underwear strengthened the DA's case, Polanski might be more willing to accept a plea bargain. On the other hand, if the underwear evidence was inconclusive, Polanski and company might prefer to take their chances with a jury. Why?

Well, first of all, perhaps Dalton, Polanski's lawyer, really thought his client was innocent. That's possible. But even if he didn't, he felt at that point he could win a complete acquittal. This was, after all, a he said/she said situation (the "he" being a beloved famous man, the "she" a not-100-percent-inexperienced kid). The medical examiner had found only semen and no sperm—meaning that a jury would hear the possibility that I, who admitted to having sexual experience, might have had that underwear stained with someone *else's* semen. More to the point, being found guilty of any of the five more serious charges could mean that Polanski would be deported. Polanski most definitely did *not* want to be deported. He loved America and Hollywood, and America and Hollywood loved him right back, blessing him with the holy trinity of success in the movies—money, power, fame. In addition, his departure would mean many people would lose their meal ticket. Polanski was making a great deal of money not only for film studios, but also for a coterie of agents and publicists. He was a one-man industry. Who'd want to see that industry flee to Europe?

That's why all the fuss over scraps of stained fabric.

. . .

In 1977, the modern victims' rights movement was still in its infancy. The first state and federal victims' rights legislation was five years away, and it was to be thirty years before California would act on it. Criminal prosecutions traditionally involved just three parties: the state government, represented by the judge who would judiciously apply the law; the people of the state, represented by the prosecution advocating for a guilty verdict and punishment for the accused; and the defense, advocating for finding the accused innocent. All parties seemed to be doing their jobs. Of course, I was oblivious to all this at the time. It only occurred to me years later that there was a greater significance to what we were doing in my case. We wanted to get recognition for a fourth party—the victim. Mine was a weak voice among the powerful parties, asking, "What about me?"

The prosecutor, Assistant District Attorney Roger Gunson, was a sensitive and straightforward man. But he had one mission—to convict Roman Polanski. The defense, led by attorney Douglas Dalton, similarly had only one goal: to get their client off. Their strategy seemed to be to establish reasonable doubt. The trial would pit Gunson, trying to prove that Roman Polanski was guilty of the rape of a thirteen-year-old girl, against Dalton, trying to establish reasonable doubt of Polanski's guilt by showing weakness in the prosecution's case. Pulling the strings was Judge Rittenband, basking in the spotlight. And at the center . . . me.

I was an uneasy participant for all concerned: a crime victim, and an uncooperative witness for the prosecution. My parents' judgment—and I couldn't agree more—was that given my attitude toward the case, I would be more damaged by the proceeding of a trial. None of us wanted me to grow up being the focus of an international sex scandal, and all I wanted was a "normal" life, or at least a chance at one. It was Larry's job to get me that chance.

We all understood that avoiding a trial meant Polanski would get off with a minor punishment for this major crime but we were clear where our priorities were. Traditional ideas of justice or biblical retribution were moot. My family and I simply wanted him to admit what he'd done, and then vanish from our lives. I figured by this time, he was already pretty damn sorry he'd done it.

Whatever it cost for me to go back to being a normal young teenager . . . that was enough justice for me.

Larry first proposed the plea bargain idea to Roger Gunson. The assistant DA was sensitive to our concerns and open to the idea, but clearly preferred to try the case. I'm not sure what his reasons were—he might have been eager to try such a high-profile case, he may have been feeling pressure from his superiors, or he may have simply believed it was the right thing to do. Perhaps it was a combination of all three. At that time, he was unwilling to commit to the particular details of a plea bargain. Larry then approached Douglas Dalton about it. He listened to Larry and responded in his usual quiet, formal way that he would consider it. But Larry was getting the message that Dalton was not interested. Perhaps Dalton thought he could create a stronger bargaining position by being non-committal. Or perhaps he thought he could sew doubt in the court's mind by destroying my credibility.

The challenge was compounded because the district attorney had just announced, after some public criticism of past plea bargains, that there were to be new standards under which they could be considered. The new plea bargain prescription was intended to give the appearance that District Attorney John Van de Kamp was being tough on crime. Now a defendant had to plead guilty to the charge that would result in the maximum amount of jail time.

Thus the timing for a high-profile plea bargain couldn't have been worse.

Two weeks and two days after my panties had been cut (the estimated time Dalton said it would take to get the forensic results from his expert), Dalton called Larry to discuss the plea bargain. Attorneys can be on opposing sides of a case and still like and respect each other. That was not true of Dalton and Larry. They were like two gladiators circling in a fight to the death. I never doubted that Larry had anything but my best interests in mind, but I know he also liked the idea of crushing Dalton. It was Dalton, not Roman, who was asking about my sexual history and questioning my mental health.

There is still a certain amount of mystery attached to the results of these tests. After two weeks, Dalton must have had them, but he never said anything to Larry. The test results of the prosecution's sample were positive for semen but negative for sperm. The semen could have possibly belonged to someone else. Sperm may have provided a clearer link to Polanski. Still, after presumably getting the results of *his* sample back, Dalton wanted to discuss a plea bargain. Is it possible that somehow sperm had been found in that portion of the sample? Perhaps the defense's test results made this less of a he said/she said situation after all.

Whatever his reasons, Dalton told Larry that Polanski would be interested in a plea bargain—but only one that would avoid prison time or deportation. There was only one of the charges that fit that requirement—the comparatively mild "unlawful sexual intercourse," previously known as "statutory rape." Rape by use of drugs and alcohol, and furnishing a controlled substance to a minor, are serious crimes that fall under the rubric of "moral turpitude" and would mandate not only jail time, but deportation. The concept of "moral turpitude" is that some crimes are such a violation of moral standards that their inherent vileness and depravity make them more serious. "Unlawful sexual intercourse" was not considered moral turpitude. Dalton said that if all the other charges were dropped, his client might be interested in pleading guilty to that single charge. Sometime later, Dalton said that the reason the prosecution had dropped all of the other charges was that they could not prove them. You have to hand it to Dalton. Even when he lost, he kept saying he'd won.

Larry then contacted Gunson. Gunson told him he had to speak to "downtown." Supervision of the matter was assigned to Chief Deputy District Attorney Stephen Trott. Gunson told Larry that Trott was not willing to accept such a plea bargain, and that it was especially problematic to accept a plea bargain in what was basically the first high-profile case since the district attorney had adopted the new, tough plea bargain guidelines. We'd thought there might be some resistance, but not a flat no.

Larry called Trott to discuss it further, and found him not just resistant but hostile. Trott's position was simply that Polanski had engaged in serious criminal conduct and that the district attorney was not willing to allow him to go forward with the least significant crime and the least significant consequences. When Larry reported this to my mother and father, they were, of course, upset and angry. To them, I was being sacrificed so that the DA could score points.

Larry felt he had only one option. He knew the prosecution needed me in court to make their case. At this time, I was across the country in my father's home in Pennsylvania. The prosecutor's office did not know where I was. So Larry started talking about me as an uncooperative witness. It was possible that I could stay in York, continuing school there and not returning to Los Angeles. Or I could go to another place beyond the reach of the California courts.

Larry informed Trott that out of concern for my best interests, I would not be cooperating further with the prosecution, and indeed would not appear at the trial. Larry was not afraid of a little saber rattling. He told Trott he thought it was a serious crime to put me through this ordeal, and that he would do everything in his power to prevent me from being forced to testify. Trott groaned. He got the message loud and clear.

It was only a few days later when Larry got the call from Roger Gunson asking if, in light of my almost certain refusal to cooperate, Larry would be willing to protect my interests and accept Polanski's guilty plea to the lesser charge. Larry's request was critical. Without formal request given to the judge in open court, they would not negotiate the guilty plea. But if Larry were willing to request the acceptance of a plea, then the district attorney would do so as well.

We had our deal.

Larry called Dalton to confirm that his client would be willing to plead guilty to unlawful sexual intercourse. Dalton took his time, but eventually agreed. Larry then called Gunson to confirm that we had a plea bargain. And because the crime was unlawful sexual intercourse, there would be probation, but no jail time. There was no way to know how the judge would react, but now we three parties—the prosecution, the defense, and the victim—wanted the same thing.

In order to get the prosecution to accept the plea bargain, Larry had agreed to read a statement to the judge urging the variation from Van de Kamp's newly articulated plea agreement rules. He read his letter, excerpted here, to Judge Rittenband in open court.

. . . My primary concern is the present and future well-being of this girl and her family. Up to this point the identity of my clients has been protected from public disclosure evincing a laudable exercise of restraint by the press. Your Honor has been sensitive to my clients' right to privacy and has protected and will protect those rights consistent with Article I, section 1 of California's Constitution, and the public policy expressed by the Legislature in its various enactments in protection of juveniles. Of course, if there were a trial in this case, the anonymity of my clients would be at an end.

In all cases, balances have to be struck. In this case, the balance that has to be affected is between the interests of society as represented by the District Attorney, the defendant, and my clients.

In evaluating my clients' interests, I am mindful that they, and more particularly she, have been harmed as the victim of unlawful acts committed by the defendant. By a trial, the integrity of the charges they preferred would have been vindicated, even though the personal cost to them would be substantial. My view, based upon advice from experts, and the view of the girl's parents, is that such a trial may cause serious damage to her. Long before I had met any other attorney in this case, my clients informed me that their goal in pressing the charges did not include seeking the incarceration of the defendant, but rather, the admission by him of wrongdoing and commencement by him, under the supervision of the court, of a program to ensure complete rehabilitation. The plea of guilty by the defendant is contrition sufficient for my clients to believe that goal may be achievable. The plea in this case has not changed the original goals and I commend them to Your Honor for consideration.

. . . Whatever harm has come to her as a victim would be exacerbated in the extreme if this case went to trial. The reliving of the sorry events with their delicate content, through the vehicle of direct and cross-examination in this courtroom packed with strangers would be a challenge to the emotional well-being of any person. The potential for harm is even greater to one of tender years. In the ordinary case, this consideration should cause concern; however, this is not the ordinary case. Although Your Honor has and would diligently protect the decorum of the courtroom, the intense national and international attention generated by this case has packed the corridors leading to and from the courtroom with a mass of media technicians flashing and prodding their equipment to feed an unseemly curiosity. A member of the media last Friday in anticipation said this case "promised to be one of the most sensational Hollywood trials . . ." This is not the place for a recovering young girl.

The public disclosure of her identity in such a charged atmosphere can only seriously harm her. Relationships with friends and indeed her family would never be the same. A stigma would attach to her for a lifetime. Justice is not made of such stuff. . . .

Judge Rittenband accepted the plea. It wasn't a perfect solution—Polanski "walked" on the most serious charges—but it was a win for me.

At the end of the proceedings Polanski stood for the traditional on-the-record plea, admitting his guilt to the charge of unlawful sexual intercourse. Polanski knew the questions that were coming and Gunson knew the answers.

"I had intercourse with a female person, not my wife, who was under eighteen years of age," Roman said.

"How old did you think the girl was?"

"I understood she was thirteen."

It was that simple. That's how this sordid affair should have ended.

But the judge wasn't through with it yet, not by a long shot.

CHAPTER 12

POLANSKI PLEADS GUILTY TO SEX CHARGE
INVOLVING TEENAGED GIRL

SANTA MONICA, Calif. (UPI): Film director Roman Polanski pleaded guilty Monday to "Unlawful sexual intercourse" with a 13-year-old girl and was ordered to undergo psychiatric examination to determine whether he should be committed to a hospital as a "mentally disordered sex offender."

Superior Court Judge Laurence J. Rittenband withheld sentencing pending a probation report on the 43-year-old former husband of murdered actress Sharon Tate and maker of such movies as "Rosemary's Baby" and "Chinatown." . . .

The district attorney's office agreed, in return for the guilty plea, to drop five other more serious counts in the indictment involving the alleged drugging and raping of the unidentified girl March 10 at the home of actor Jack Nicholson, who was away at the time. . . .

. . . District Attorney John Van De Kamp said the "plea bargaining arrangement was reached largely at the urging of the girl's family that she be spared the ordeal of appearing on the witness stand at a sensational trial."

. . .

In California, whenever a defendant in a felony case is convicted of a crime, whether it's for a plea bargain or a jury verdict, a probation report is prepared. The report includes a number of different elements, among them a description of the circumstances of the crime; the person's family and work history; a psychological evaluation; and a recommended sentence. The idea is to help the judge decide a proper sentence for the defendant.

But the probation report does not dictate what a judge must do—and in this case, it was hard to predict what Judge Rittenband would do one day to the next, or one ruling to the next. His decisions and reactions depended on any number of things, and looking back it seems they mostly had to do with his ego. At some point, this unpredictability turned into something that looked more like instability.

One thing was clear: the judge wasn't much interested in me. For him, this case was all about power and publicity, and Mom and I were inconsequential nuisances. He wasn't exactly shy about revealing his true feelings for us. At one memorable hearing, with the defense floating the theory that my mother had foisted me off on Polanski to advance her own career, he said, "What do we have here, a mother/daughter hooker team?"

Still, it seemed everyone was in agreement. My mother, father, Larry, and I agreed—and still do with the probation report's final recommendation, that Polanski's sentence be probation and nothing more. But here's where things got even trickier with Judge Rittenband, who seemed to be having a grand old time at the center of the media spotlight.

The judge summoned Larry, Gunson, and Dalton to his office and said it would reflect poorly on him—Judge Rittenband—if he were to let Roman off without so much as a day in jail. Public scrutiny of this case had simply been too great, and Rittenband risked looking like a wuss if Polanski, who had just signed on to do a film in Bora-Bora with Dino De Laurentiis, got only probation.

Larry told us there had been hallway murmuring at the courthouse that the judge had solicited opinions and recommendations of reporters, trying to gauge how the media would react to one decision or another and how he, the judge, would be viewed. No one would come out and openly accuse the judge of such improprieties, but now here he was flatly admitting he was weighing public and press opinion in his sentencing decision. Incredible.

This is the convoluted solution he arrived at: He would send Polanski to Chino State Prison for ninety days, for something called a "diagnostic study." Both Gunson and Dalton protested. Gunson pointed out to the judge that under the law, a study of this kind could not be used as punishment, and Dalton said that this step went against everything the judge had indicated he would do. Dalton also said that his client was about to embark on a new film project that would last about a year.

But the judge said not to worry. He was going to sentence him, but well, not really. In order to make each lawyer happy and to protect his image as a tough-minded defender of justice, Judge Rittenband planned some stage direction of his own.

When we get into court, here's what I want you to do, he told the lawyers. He told Gunson to argue that he wanted Polanski put in custody. Then, he said, he would speak from the bench before issuing the ninety-day sentence. That would be Dalton's cue to speak, but under backstage directions from the judge, Dalton was not permitted to argue the punishment was too harsh.

Well, this *was* Hollywood. Judge Rittenband had cast himself as writer-director-producer-actor and was orchestrating every beat of this production, thinking only about what was best for his own image. My family was only concerned that I did not get called to testify. That's why we agreed to—*encouraged*—the reduced charges, but we still wanted all parts of the agreement to be enforced. If the judge changed one part, the rest of the agreement could fall apart and I'd find myself on the stand being cross-examined by Douglas Dalton.

The public would know there had been a plea bargain, that Polanski had admitted to unlawful sexual intercourse, and that he was sentenced to Chino State Prison for ninety days for a diagnostic study with the chance, depending on the results of that study, he could be sentenced to more time. Here's what the public would not know—that the judge had offered Dalton a deal. He would sentence Roman to ninety days, but Dalton would ask for deferrals in ninety-day increments. In a year's time, when all had calmed, and additional favorable probation reports had come in, the judge would make the whole business go away. No one in the media or the public would be the wiser.

Larry understood that Dalton had no choice. He had to either play it the judge's way or risk the collapse of the plea deal altogether. There was no reasoned approach with Judge Rittenband, the lawyers were now fully realizing, not with someone far more interested in the movie starring Laurence Rittenband than in the movie starring Polanski and a thirteen-year-old rape victim.

And so the lawyers walked into court, resigned to saying their lines as the judge had directed. First Gunson, then Judge Rittenband, then Dalton, then Larry. Curtain. Applause.

If nothing else, the judge's trespasses forged some unusual alliances, between the antagonists Larry and Dalton, and between the natural adversaries Dalton and Gunson. They may have had problems with each other personally, but they bonded over their shared sense that Rittenband was certifiable.

Rittenband had asked Polanski to give an accounting of himself. It is affecting in its very coolness; he had lived through a great deal. It says in part:

Dear Judge Rittenband,

I have been asked to write you a short account of my life. Following is what I think are the chief things that have happened to me. . . .

I was born in Paris in 1933, of Polish immigrants who had met and married in Paris. Shortly before the war, their financial situation forced our return to Poland. In September, 1939, I started school in Cracow, but after one week the war began. We fled to Warsaw, hoping and believing the Germans would never advance that far. Unfortunately, the city was destroyed and the country fell.

We returned to occupied Cracow and were soon segregated with the rest of the Jewish population. I don't think I need dwell too much on the known events of the next few years. The population of the ghetto was systematically reduced by raids. . . .

Presently my mother was taken to Auschwitz, where she died. It wasn't until long after the war that I learnt she was pregnant. Before one raid, I cut through the barbed wire as usual but when I sneaked back I discovered that this time it was the final liquidation of our Cracow ghetto. The last men were being marched away, including my father. I tried to speak to him, but he signaled me to run away, which I managed to do. I was eight years old at the time.

Somehow I managed to survive the next few years, moving between various friends of my family and relatives in isolated parts of the country. Occasionally I ventured into town and sold newspapers, and my chief memory here is of going to movies with the money I made from that. I felt a slight guilt at this, because the movies were German and patriotic slogans on the wall said: "Only pigs go to movies."

The Soviet offensive of 1945 found me back in Cracow, and after the liberation I remained there, unhurt by the war except for an arm injury caused by the very last bombs dropped by the retreating Germans. An uncle found me in the street and took me in.

A few months later my father returned from Mauthausen, which he had miraculously survived. I was naturally overcome with joy, but then he remarried, and for some reason that neither of us ever fully understood and made both of us sad, we were never again as close as we had been during my earliest childhood. It seemed best that he give me an allowance and that I live from then on in a kind of boarding house.

Now I'm thirteen, back in school. I started working on the side as a child actor, and at fourteen I played the lead in a play called "Son of the Regiment." It was a big smash, and unquestionably the acclaim I received determined my desire to follow a theatrical career. My interest in school academics lessened. I became a poor student at best, though I vigorously pursued athletics of all kinds, specially bicycle racing. Probably my small stature, of which children are terribly conscious even if they don't say so, was a powerful motivation towards those physical activities, which indeed I have pursued to the present day.

At sixteen I was attacked by a thug trying to rob me. He beat me on the head with a stone hard enough to put me in hospital for two weeks, with another month in bed recuperation. Actually, I was luckier than I realized. The thug was arrested and found guilty of

murdering three persons during assaults similar to the one on me.
He was hanged.

[Eventually Polanski ended up in Poland's National Film
School, married, and in 1960 was able to make his first feature
film, *Knife in the Water.* His wife left him, he moved to France,
and he eventually spent time in London also making movies,
despite barely speaking English.]

Soon after, Robert Evans of Paramount Pictures invited me to
Hollywood in 1967 to make my first American movie: "Rosemary's
Baby." It wasn't surprising: I was already typed as a horror-movie
director because of "Repulsion." I had never specially intended to
concentrate on that genre—it had simply seemed the most saleable
when I was broke—but as so often seems to happen, accidental
choices turn into the back-stories that color the rest of our lives.

I married Sharon in 1968 in London, though we'd already de-
cided to live in California. "Rosemary's Baby" was an enormous
hit. Everything seemed to be working out.

Then came the events of 1969 which made everything that I
achieved seem senseless and futile. California became unbearable
after that. I returned to London to live and work. Though I threw
myself into professional activity with all my energy, my next two
pictures, "Macbeth" and "What?" turned out to be failures. In
1973, Robert Evans invited me once more to Hollywood, this time
to make the film "Chinatown."

I was filled with apprehension about coming back to Califor-

nia, but the plain truth is that I needed the money—also, a successful picture, if I were to survive in my profession. Once I started work, everything went well. "Chinatown" was released in 1974 and received eleven nominations for the Academy Awards. . . .

[But a] strange tainted reputation seemed to accompany me, based partly on the subject matter of my films but even more so on the enormous publicity given Sharon's murder. I was welcomed everywhere as a "jet-setter" and given unending parties. I found it harder and harder to establish meaningful relationships with women. . . .

[Polanski goes on to detail a series of career setbacks.]

That is where I was on March 11th of this year, when once again the circumstances of my life changed completely. The Columbia project was cancelled. My Italian investors in "Pirates" took the well-reported charges against me as a signal that they should bring a huge civil action against me for recovery of their advances, an action which is still pending.

Notwithstanding all these things, the producer Dino De Laurentiis offered me a new project, "The Hurricane," in late May, which I accepted with gratitude and enthusiasm, and on which I am now working. He was only able to make me this offer at such a time because he is a genuine independent, answerable to no stockholders. In accordance with his trust in me, he has already committed lots of money to many, many people who will work with me on "The Hurricane."

I hope circumstances don't prevent me from justifying and re-paying that trust.

If you have any further questions, I'll certainly do my best to answer them.

Sincerely yours,

Roman Polanski

Polanski's assessment of himself was at least not mawkish or self-pitying. But the probation report of acting probation officer Kenneth F. Faye (and signed by a deputy, Irwin Gold) seemed to be recommending Polanski for the Nobel Peace Prize—or at the very least the Oscars' Jean Hersholt Humanitarian Award.

First, the report detailed Polanski's early suffering and the tragic death of his wife, noting that Polanski never saw a psychiatrist because he worried it "could interfere with the creative process." He allowed that Polanski exercised "transient poor judgment and loss of normal inhibitions in circumstances of intimacy and collaboration in creative work, with some coincidental alcohol and drug intoxication" (the Quaaludes, he explained with not a trace of skepticism, had been prescribed to him for jet lag). He then went on to describe the "physical maturity and willingness and provocativeness of the victim, and the lack of coercion by the defendant and his solicitude concerning pregnancy." (An interesting new euphemism for sodomy, apparently.) Despite my age and testimony that I had objected to having sex with Polanski and that I had asked to leave, the report concluded, "There was some indication that circumstances were provocative, that there was some permissiveness by the mother." In other words, the "mother-daughter hooker team," as Rittenband had labeled us. "Incarceration," he wrote, "would impose an unusual degree of stress and hardship because of his highly sensitive personality."

But that wasn't enough. The probation report included assessments by psychiatrists drawn, it seems, from the Roman Polanski Fan Club. One seemed to fancy himself a film critic. "The defendant has not only survived, he has prevailed . . . and has become one of the leading creative forces of the last two decades. . . . Possibly not since Renaissance Italy has there been such a gathering of creative minds in the locale as there has been in Los Angeles County during the past half century . . . while they have brought with them the manners and mores of their native lands which in rare instances have been at variance with those of their adoptive lands."

Don't blame the man; blame the (foreign) culture.

The *New York Times* reported:

One psychiatrist who examined Mr. Polanski, Alvin E. Davis, found he was not mentally ill or disordered, and not "a sexual deviate." "He is of superior intelligence, has good judgment and strong moral and ethical values," the report said of Dr. Davis's conclusions.

"He is not a pedophile," Dr. Davis is quoted as saying. "The offense occurred as an isolated instance of transient poor judgment

and loss of normal inhibitions in circumstances of intimacy and collaboration in creative work, and with some coincidental alcohol and drug intoxication."

The probation report concluded: "It is believed that incalculable emotional damage could result from incarcerating the defendant whose own life has been a seemingly unending series of punishments."

The letters of support from friends, too, tended to indirectly cast doubt on his thirteen-year-old victim and her motives. You could see the White Male 1970s Guys circling the wagons.

"There is, in fact, very little that is dark or sinister about Roman," said Gene Gutowski, the producer of many of Polanski's most acclaimed films. "He has remained amazingly normal and well adjusted . . . generous to a fault, uninterested in material gains of possession, he is a loyal and kind friend, thoughtful, and completely trusting, possibly excessively so. As a result, he has been used from time to time by young and ambitious females who felt that being seen with Roman in public or having their names linked with his in the gossip columns would lead to their advancement or gain them publicity."

Producer Robert Evans, Paramount Pictures: "I know the suffering that has gone into his life, especially these last ten years, and I feel that [the press] has maligned him terribly. He may make for provocative headlines, but with rare exception, the press has never captured the beauty of Roman's soul."

And perhaps most tellingly, director and producer Howard

Koch: "I'm sure the situation he finds himself in now is one of those things that could happen to any one of us."

Incidentally, the hosannas didn't come only from men in Hollywood. Fifteen years before she discovered that Woody Allen had nude photographs of her daughter, Mia Farrow also publicly supported Polanski.

As I said, my family and I didn't care if Polanski was imprisoned. There was no value to be gained in that, and we weren't vindictive. But to see the empathy that was extended his way, while virtually none was offered to us, was a very sobering thing. The report referred in passing to hate mail he received, but it also cited a letter of support for Polanski that read, "We should all help him get well for we are in his debt due to his artistry. . . . We should not cast him out of our society."

As for Judge Rittenband, he quickly held a news conference in his chambers to explain the sentencing. In all of Larry's experience, before or since, he had never heard of a judge so obsessed with his public profile that he actually conducted a question-and-answer session with the press. The case seemed to be moving to another phase, but Judge Rittenband was determined not to relinquish center stage so easily.

So with the sentence to undergo the "diagnostic study" for ninety days in Chino State Prison in place and seemingly press-approved, Judge Rittenband gave Polanski the ninety-day stay to finish preproduction work on a movie for Dino De Laurentiis's, *Hurricane.* Polanski's devil-may-care attitude displayed during this furlough proved to be his undoing.

The director was supposed to be heading to Bora-Bora for preproduction. Instead, he stopped in Germany to try to set up a distribution deal and check on some casting possibilities— including his former lover Nastassja Kinski. (The film eventually starred Mia Farrow, Jason Robards as the marauding white oppressor, and some guy who looked great without a shirt as the Culturally Pure Native. There's a lot of bad weather. That's all you need to know.) Polanski happened to be in Munich during Oktoberfest—and he was never one to shun a party.

The *Santa Monica Evening Outlook* ran a UPI photo of him surrounded by a bevy of young, attractive fräuleins, with the caption, "Film Director Roman Polanski, who was given a stay of a Santa Monica Superior Court order that he undergo a 90 day diagnostic study at a State prison, puffs at a cigar as he enjoys the companionship of some young ladies at the Munich, Germany Oktoberfest."

While Polanski protested that the photo had been cropped, and in fact all the women surrounding him were also surrounded by their husbands and boyfriends, it was too late. Rittenband was seething. He was being played the fool, he said, and told a reporter from the *Los Angeles Herald Examiner* that "Roman Polanski could be on his way to prison this weekend," adding, "I didn't know when I let him go that the movie would be impossible to finish in 90 days. I do feel that I have very possibly been imposed upon."

Polanski, at Judge Rittenband's orders, returned, and when he did, the judge gave him the ninety days for that diagnostic study. Predictably, this was all accompanied by another media scramble and more debate about whether Polanski was getting his just rewards or was the victim of persecution. Judge Rittenband angrily let it be known to the lawyers that he alone held Polanski's fate in his hands, that he still had the power to put him away for fifty years.

On December 16—after a farewell bash attended by Tony Richardson, Jack Nicholson, and Kenneth Tynan, among others—Polanski was escorted through a phalanx of photographers and reporters to the state prison by his entertainment lawyer, Wally Wolf, and Hercules Bellville, his friend and second unit director on several of his films. Polanski believed Judge Rittenband, in a fit of pique, tipped the media off as to the date and time of his arrival.

Years later, in his autobiography, Polanski claimed he actually found a certain contentment in jail, and while various stories leaked into the rags courtesy of other on-the-take inmates (including a story that he'd promised a prisoner's four-year-old daughter a part in his next movie, with a sinister insinuation of his love for the *very* young), the time he passed there was relatively trouble-free. "I felt secure and at peace," he wrote.

CHAPTER 13

At the beginning of tenth grade, everything was wrong. Everything. First and most important, I was back in California, back where I was The Girl, missing my friends and boyfriend back in York. I was in a new high school where I knew virtually no one, since my junior high friends had dispersed to other schools. I wasn't friends with the popular girls, whom we called the Guccis. (The designer of the moment; you had to have those jeans, plus the gold chains and hoop earrings, or you were nothing.) I cut my hair short and gained some weight; I told myself I wanted a different look—and I did—but I also had some ideas about looking tougher. It had always been easy for me to get good grades, but now the grades meant nothing. I became cozy with the stoners—a low-pressure group of kids who never asked me any questions, partially because they didn't know about what had happened over the past year, but also because they didn't care. In some sense we were losing ourselves in drugs, but still finding great solace in each other.

My mother was constantly worried about me, but felt powerless to help. As she told me many years later, her attitude toward me at the time was "What can I do for you? Can I give you more? How can I make you happy?" It was total, total, guilt.

I don't think this escalation of acting out was a conscious choice, but I was angry at the world and, with any thoughts of becoming an actress dashed, I didn't want to be a cute little child anymore.

Not that I had to worry there. Before we learned there wouldn't be a trial, my mother was very worried: I had grown and looked a lot older in the course of the year, and she felt that while I looked younger than thirteen at the time of the assault I really could now be mistaken for a teenager who was at least sixteen or seventeen. This would make the press even more hostile and would make it more believable that Polanski assumed I was of age.

I became more easily upset about everything, and spent a great deal of time crying in my bedroom. I didn't want to be in California, I didn't want to be in school . . . I just wanted to get off this train to Crazytown.

When my mother told me Polanski was locked up in jail undergoing psychiatric evaluation, I didn't feel the slightest sense of satisfaction or justice served. To the contrary. I wished no one had ever found out. I continually kept second-guessing myself about that night. Why didn't I put up more of a fight? Why did I drink? Why did I take the Quaalude? I felt certain I could have made him stop. I know it wasn't rational but I felt responsible for it all. After months of this I came to see that blaming myself was wrong and useless, so I decided to sort of put these feelings aside, lock them in a box. When Mom told me about Polanski, I nodded and just walked away.

I was determined to get on with life. But it would become a life of "look away."

. . .

Polanski was released from Chino State Prison on January 29, 1978, after having served forty-two days. The psychiatric report from Chino was, if anything, even more flattering than the original probation report. I'm sure he was an exemplary prisoner. Yet it's pretty clear the prison officials were no more immune to the power of celebrity than the average groupie.

Philip S. Wagner, Chino's chief psychiatrist, portrayed prisoner Polanski as more the victim than the violator. "There was no evidence that the offense was in any way characterized by destructive or insensitive attitude toward the victim," he wrote. "Polanski's attitude was undoubtedly seductive, but considerate. The relationship with his victim developed from an attitude of professional, to playful mutual eroticism. . . . Polanski seems to have been unaware at the time that he was involving himself in a criminal offense, an isolated instance of naiveté, unusual in a mature, sophisticated man."

It's not that I disagreed with much of that statement . . . but "*mutual* eroticism"? "Isolated instance of naiveté"? Please.

When officials at Chino released Polanski less than half-way through his ninety-day "sentence" and said the diagnostic study was complete, the press was not happy. And when the press was unhappy, so was Rittenband. He called the lawyers back to his chambers for one more wild ride.

Larry had no formal role in the ensuing negotiations, but he was there, as he would say, to bring a conscience to all the mayhem—to remind them that there was a girl whose entire life could be affected by their decisions. On January 31, 1978, the day before Roman was scheduled to return to Judge Rittenband's courtroom, the lawyers answered the judge's summons. As usual, Gunson and Dalton took the two seats in front of Rittenband's desk, and Larry took his place at the side of the large desk, next to the judge.

Larry recalls that Judge Rittenband began angrily and pompously lecturing them about how he wouldn't allow Polanski to make a mockery of the courts. When his intercom buzzed, Rittenband growled to his secretary that he had directed her not to interrupt him under any circumstances and now she was interrupting him.

"Sir," she said, over the intercom, "Bill Farr is on the phone."

William Farr was a youngish (now deceased) reporter for the *Los Angeles Times,* and he'd been following the case. Known among fellow journalists for his gutsiness—he had served jail time during the Manson trial for refusing to disclose a source in one of his articles on the family that revealed they were plotting to kill Elizabeth Taylor and Frank Sinatra—he was also apparently a confidant of Rittenband. When Farr called, the conversation between the judge and Gunson and Dalton halted. "Yes," he said. "I'll take the call."

Gunson and Dalton whispered to one another so as not to interfere with Rittenband's phone call. Larry (as he explained to me later) couldn't take part in their conversation where he was seated, so short of leaving the room or putting his fingers in his ears, he couldn't help but hear the conversation between Farr and Rittenband. It sounded to Larry that they were involved in some kind of high-level decision making—but how could that be? One person on the call was the judge who ruled over the case, and the other person was a reporter.

"No! No! No! I'm going to do what I told you I would, and I'm going to stick to it," Judge Rittenband said. "No, I haven't told the lawyers yet!"

Gunson and Dalton, sitting there with nothing to do, shifted awkwardly in their seats. They couldn't hear what the judge was saying into the phone, and had no idea what was going on. Larry was flabbergasted. Rittenband was getting advice from a reporter? Why? It's one thing to play *to* the media; it's quite another to be played *by* the media. It was also clear to Larry that Rittenband and Farr were continuing a conversation begun at another time.

Judge Rittenband's phone session went on for a half hour. The lawyers continued to sit and wait. The judge displayed no self-consciousness over what he was doing. If anything, he seemed to be showing off for the attorneys a little bit: *These press guys, they can't get enough of me!* On top of that, he was more concerned about the reporter's needs than the needs of the lawyers. "I'm not going to take it under advisement," he said. "I'll announce it from the bench tomorrow and you can meet your deadline."

Larry could hear Farr's voice, but couldn't make out what he was telling the judge.

Louder now so that Gunson and Dalton could hear, Rittenband went on: "I'm not doing that because if I did that I'd be seriously criticized by everybody and I'm not going to be criticized for helping him."

The dumbfounded lawyers looked at each other. Was he really having this conversation in front of them?

Fearing press criticism, Rittenband was changing course once again. The forty-two days were not enough. He decided instead he was going to give Polanski an indeterminate sentence. That means exactly what it sounds like: the duration of the sentence is not spelled out. It could be a week. It could be fifty years.

Seeing the incredulous looks on the attorneys' faces, Rittenband hastened to reassure them: "Don't be concerned about that," he said. "I want people to think I'm a tough sentencer. So we'll do this, and when the attention is off the case, you"—indicating Dalton—"petition for a change of sentence and I will sentence him to time served. I'll put this forth tomorrow."

They were stunned. Polanski had glowing probation reports. Rittenband had *already* agreed to time served. Then, with a little media heat and the tut-tutting of one reporter, the judge was changing his mind.

These days, anyone convicted of "unlawful sexual intercourse" could serve a maximum of four years (not that those convicted served nearly that much, even then; the sentence was generally six months or less). But back in 1978, a sentence of fifty years was theoretically possible. If the parties agreed to an indeterminate sentence, Roman Polanski could, at the judge's whim, end up in jail for the rest of his life.

Dalton, Gunson, and Larry walked numbly to the courthouse coffee shop and ordered coffee. After a long silence, Dalton turned to Gunson and asked, "Should I trust him?" Gunson shot him a look. "Oh, I don't see why not," he said, dryly. "You trusted him before."

Dalton looked tired. "I have a client who is sitting in my office waiting for me to let him know what happened. I better tell him." He walked to the pay phone. He talked to his client.

As Polanski told the story later, there was one seat left on that afternoon's British Airways flight to Heathrow. He bought it.

PART THREE

CHAPTER 14

POLANSKI FLEES TO PARIS

Jacksonville (Ill.) Courier

February 2, 1978

LONDON (AP): The London Evening News reported it located film director Roman Polanski at his Paris home following his flight from California to escape sentencing for having sexual relations with a 13-year-old girl. His extradition to the United States appears unlikely.

The Evening News said a manservant at Polanski's residence in the French capital told its reporter: "Yes, Mr. Polanski arrived here this morning. He is very tired and is resting quietly. He's not ill, just tired."

The 44-year-old director of "Rosemary's Baby" and "Chinatown" arrived at London's Heathrow Airport Wednesday morning on a British airliner from Los Angeles, but reporters were unable to locate him afterward.

Scotland Yard said it was not looking for him.

"He has committed no crime in Britain, and as far as I know we have not received any message from America about him," a spokesman for the Yard said.

Polanski is a French citizen, reportedly with homes in both London and Paris, and the prosecutor handling his case in California suggested he was headed for France, where he would be safe from extradition. Friends in Paris indicated they had talked with him in London but said they did not know what his plans were. French citizens cannot be extradited from France on any charge.

Polanski failed to appear for sentencing in Santa Monica, CA Wednesday. His lawyer, Douglas Dalton, announced in the packed courtroom: "I received a call from Mr. Polanski this morning advising me he would not be here. . . . I do not believe he is in the United States."

Superior Court Judge Laurence J. Rittenband issued a bench warrant for the director's arrest and granted Dalton's request for time to try to persuade him to return. The judge scheduled another hearing February 14 where he could sentence Polanski in absentia.

Dalton said he would "use every effort" to have his client return by then. . . .

On February 1, 1978—the day Polanski was supposed to appear in court and the judge was supposed to accept the plea bargain—there was a flurry of activity. Someone told Larry, "He isn't here. He took off." Larry went to Dalton and asked what was going on and Dalton, true to form, ignored him.

Then Larry asked Gunson, who said, "Polanski skipped." Larry asked what would happen. Gunson replied, "I don't know."

In court, Dalton said he'd received a call from Polanski advising him he wouldn't be there that day. Rittenband asked, "What did he tell you?" and Dalton invoked attorney/client privilege. "Did you tell [Polanski] to return and appear for sentencing?" Rittenband asked. Dalton replied, "Your Honor, I have fulfilled all my obligations."

Larry said you could almost see the steam coming out of Rittenband's ears.

At any rate, about a week later Dalton called Larry and told him he was going to file a motion to have Rittenband disqualified and asked him if he would read it and tell him if he thought the declaration was accurate. He had already asked Gunson to do the same. They both had agreed to review and respond to the draft. Rittenband's lack of professionalism was the one thing all sides could agree on.

Rittenband filed an answer to the motion, in which he disputed the conclusions and insisted he could continue to act fairly. While he didn't concede any wrongdoing, he nevertheless resigned from the case. He saved himself from being disqualified, but the effect was the same, and that was what mattered: he was off the case. For the rest of his life he never got over his fury, never acknowledged there was anything untoward about his judicial behavior. More than a decade later, when asked about Polanski's flight, the judge referenced Gilbert and Sullivan's *Mikado,* where the Lord High Executioner keeps "a little list" of prospects for beheadings, quoting, "I've got him on my list. I've got him on my list." Rittenband unfailingly scoffed at the allegations until the time of his death in 1993.

Thirty years would pass before Polanski would be charged with jumping bail or not appearing in court—and that was at the time of his arrest and attempted extradition in 2009. Roger Gunson continued to work at the DA's office until then, and he made it clear that he would not charge Polanski with those crimes.

My family was never aware of any problems with the plea deal, so it came as a surprise to my mother when Larry told her that Polanski had left the country. But after he explained what had happened, she certainly understood why. She was relieved and pleased. She thought that I had gotten what I had wanted. Once, when I was pressured to say what I thought should happen to him, I answered that I thought he should leave the country. I didn't really want anything to happen to him; it was just the only answer I could think of. When my mom told me he was gone— well, I won't call it one of the happiest days of our lives, but certainly it was the one filled with the greatest relief. The air was just a little easier to breathe. I never thought to question what had happened. All I could think was: *FREEEEEEEDOMMMMMM*. No more telling my story. No more seeing myself called "sex victim girl" in the paper. At the same time, I think I knew in my heart that someday, somehow I would have to deal with this all again. But I had about as much sense of the future as a beagle: I lived in the present, and maybe five seconds in the past and five seconds in the future. So, fine, there would be problems eventually, but for now I could get on with my life.

But what exactly *was* that life? It certainly wouldn't be acting or modeling. I could see the headlines: "Sex Victim Girl Gets Part on Sitcom." Oh well, I thought to myself. Oh well, and that was all. My life had been in a holding pattern for a year; the last thing I wanted to do was keep worrying about the future.

This was the year of Fleetwood Mac's "Don't Stop":

> *If your life was bad to you,*
> *Just think what tomorrow will do.*

The summer after tenth grade I returned to York, taking Crystal, my friend from the gymnastics team, with me. With all the excellent common sense of a stoner-in-training, I decided this was my time to let loose. Looking back, this is when my life started to unravel. Whatever drugs I could find, well, I'd do them. Whatever boys I could find, I'd do them, too. Boston came out with their anthem to moving on, "Don't Look Back." I didn't intend to.

I was out of control. Dad was understandably worried about the bad example I had become for my younger stepbrothers, and Jan (now officially my stepmother) was sick of cleaning up the mess of beer bottles and overflowing ashtrays she would find stashed in my room. I still had my boyfriend John (and sometimes Jimmy if John wasn't around), but it was my friend Joey who got me home when I was so drunk I couldn't stand:

he carried me to the porch, rang the doorbell, and fled, just in time to miss the sight of my Dad opening the door to me vomiting on his shoes. Dad wasn't happy. They were nice shoes.

My father and I had adored each other, but our relationship was never the same after Polanski. It wasn't that he blamed me in any way for the rape—he was nothing but supportive, compassionate, and, well, fatherly. But I'd gone from Daddy's little girl to this belligerent, sullen, rebel-without-a-cause, and even though he tended to blame my mother for my recklessness, I was a gigantic pain in his ass. I resented his attempts to rein me in, and he was impatient with how my unruly behavior was upsetting his happy home. He just didn't want to put up with my shit. Who would?

That summer was pretty much a harbinger of eleventh grade. By the middle of the school year, my ritual went like this: Mom would drop me off at the back door of school; I'd walk straight out the front door with Crystal; we'd take the bus to her house; we would hang out and smoke pot all day.

There were plenty of harder drugs around, too: cocaine, Quaaludes, and LSD were easy to find and I was happy to use whatever I could get my hands on. There was a lot of speed available in the Ralphs grocery store parking lot and my mother and gymnastics coach were pleased to see me lose that weight I had put on. (I was still showing up for practice, even when I wasn't showing up for classes.) Having the body image issues of any teenage girl, I wondered if they would really mind that I was on speed. Wasn't looking good and performing well more important? Eventually, I only went by school to buy drugs. By the time the administration called Mom in June to tell her I hadn't been in school since March, I had taken my equivalency test on the sly and managed to pass even though I had been up till 2:00 AM doing acid the night before. I had effectively graduated. She was disappointed, but what could she do? She knew how much I hated it, and there was no way in hell I was going back. Looking on the bright side, I had gotten moved up a grade when I started kindergarten and now I'd graduated early. I feigned interest in community college to smooth things over.

None of my friends were really bona fide drug dealers: we used most of what we bought and sold the rest to keep ourselves going. (Okay, maybe we *were* drug dealers, but not very good ones.) I smoked a lot, tripped occasionally, did a lot of speed, and moved on to cocaine and Quaaludes. I thought all of this was a hell of a good time, and so did the people I hung around with. Maybe I was trying to cope with what happened to me the year before. Or maybe not. Maybe I just liked getting high. One shouldn't overanalyze the whims of a teenage girl on drugs.

I managed to keep my life as a truant drug user hidden from my mother. To please her, and perhaps to make it appear I was fully functioning, I went on a call for a Kool-Aid commercial. I didn't feel like doing it—I just wanted to hang out with my boyfriend and party—but we'd had photos done for a new head shot and I had promised Mom I'd keep the appointment. I did a line before I went and I got the part, which taught me this oh-so-valuable lesson: people like you when you're high!

I hung out with my tight group of friends—Crystal, Brett, Craig, and Ron and a few others. We did everything together. In retrospect, I suppose it's obvious I was hiding my pain beneath a veneer of cool. Drugs were an escape, of course, but often no amount of smoking dope or cranking up Aerosmith was doing it for me.

. . .

One afternoon at Taft (my high school), my friend Ron was supposed to give me a ride home, but his friend Craig found me a ride instead. The car had more teenagers in it than seats. So my solution was to sit on Craig's lap. And thus began a relationship that would last, on and off, for the next eight years. Craig was, to put it bluntly, beautiful. He had scraggly dirty-blond hair, long sideburns, and cornflower-blue eyes. He was a perfect 1970s bad boy, kind of a sixteen-year-old Burt Reynolds. He had broken both legs in a dirt bike accident, which meant that he'd spent months in traction, lifting weights to make his upper body buff. He lived a block from me with his mother when we met. I'd heard awful stories about his father before their divorce. He was the kind of man who kept locks on the kitchen cabinets because he felt his kids ate too much. At one point he sold Craig's dirt bike, supposedly to pay for repairs to a broken door (never fixed). Another time, to teach his son some sort of lesson, he gave away Craig's dog while Craig was away for the weekend. I don't think I ever knew the dad's real name; Craig's mom just called him "Hitler."

Craig knew where to get drugs and knew that I wanted them; we got high a lot. At the same time, he was extremely competent mechanically: he could fix any car. He shot guns and rode dirt bikes, and he taught me how to do all those things, too. We would go camping in the desert to ride and shoot. Drinking/drugs/dirt bikes/guns: great combo. Once, after a day at the beach, we stopped in Malibu Canyon so I could pee by the side of the road. I got bitten by a rattlesnake while stumbling through the brush and didn't even realize it. On the plus side, though, I was with the kind of boyfriend who'd seen a lot in his short life and didn't easily panic. He got me to the hospital as the paralyzing poison steadily worked its way up my increasingly immobilized body. No problem. However irrational it was, given his taste for danger, I always felt safe with Craig.

And yet he could be a terror and he was controlling—and I was never someone who liked being controlled, even if it was for my own good. He wasn't stupid; he would get exasperated with my life goal, which, at that point, was to do as little work as possible. There was a lot of drinking and screaming and hitting—and I gave as good as I got. It had to end, and it did, several times. But we kept coming back to each other. I couldn't help myself. He was the man to me.

I'm astounded that in the next few years, nothing truly horrible happened. Nobody got arrested, and there were only two car accidents. Well, three, if you count the time I visited my sister, Kim, back in York and set her car on fire. (I'd run out of gas and found some lawn mower gas and poured it into the carburetor to get the car started and—well, all I can say is, don't do it. But . . . could have happened to anyone, right?)

Was I acting out? I never thought I was. Would I have chosen a more straight-and-narrow path if it weren't for the Polanski incident? Possibly. My mother and Bob, so riddled with guilt, were only able to say yes to me. I remember one July Fourth in particular, when Bob overheard our plans to drop acid and watch fireworks. He insisted on chaperoning us because he was concerned. (He knew that even if he stopped us that night, we'd just go and do it some other night.) He drove us in the back of his truck up to the hills above the house to watch the fireworks, and made sure we got home safe. Little did he know, we were dropping acid all the time. This just happened to be a particularly festive night to do it.

You could call Mom and Bob enablers, but that's sort of like calling forest rangers who start a controlled burn before wildfire season "enablers." No; the rangers want to minimize inevitable damage. So did Mom and Bob. As outrageous as I could be sometimes, I always felt cared for. I think I would have gotten into a lot more trouble without them.

My father had been the only person who cared about my academic performance. But by this point even he had given up on having an academically inclined daughter. "You should go to college to meet a man who'll take care of you," he said. I didn't listen, but he was right. Over the next ten years, if there had been an Olympics for job-quitting, I would have won the gold. I was extremely adept at *getting* jobs, because I was smart and capable. But then, generally, I quit before I got fired. Our relationship gradually deteriorated. He could be particularly cold and mean when he was drinking. In an effort to dissuade me from an acting career he once said to me, "There must be a hundred girls within a twenty-mile radius of your house that have more talent and are better-looking than you."

Craig and I had moved in together in 1980, when I was seventeen. By the following summer I'd had enough. I decided to make a break from California and from Craig. I packed up my stuff in my Camaro, unloaded it back at Mom's, left a note on my desk at work, and got on a plane back to York. Staying with Dad wasn't an option at that point, so I went to stay with my sister at her farm, outside of town. It was another summer of partying, getting high, watching the band practice in the abandoned skate park, staying out all night, sleeping all day, and trying to find the odd job to pay for beer and food. I wasn't making it work, so I finally headed back to California again. After I got back, I did various jobs—bank teller, payroll clerk, clothing retail—and I was bored out of my mind with all of them. During that time I began seeing a ruggedly handsome boy named Rex, who, I decided, was my ticket out of everything. Or more specifically, Rex and the baby I was carrying—because very soon after we began seeing each other I got pregnant. It would be fine, I thought; Rex would take care of me and the baby. I walked down the aisle in my gunnysack dress on May 8, 1982; my dad gave me away. Jes was born that November. Ten months later, after one too many incidents where Rex wasn't where he said he'd be, we separated. Many years have passed, and Rex has turned out to be a great man and great father. But at the time he was nineteen. He was stuck with a pregnant wife, while the other guys were out having fun. Now that I had a baby, I wanted to stay home, but I had to find a way to take care of Jes and myself. So I did babysitting for neighbors in my home until he was old enough for preschool.

And here's the thing. As immature as my thinking was at the time (Hey, I know what will be easier than working— a baby!), having Jes really did save my life. My life began to have responsibility and purpose. At the same time, my friends were beginning to use harder drugs. Free-basing was the latest thing, and that had consequences. Consequences like arrest, addiction. There are some things no girl should have to do to fund a habit. I knew people who did those things.

Having a baby was not really compatible with that lifestyle, so I stopped everything but the occasional joint or beer. After Rex and I split, I lived at home with Mom but more or less spent every night with Craig, whom I'd gotten back together with and who only lived a mile away. Jes was like everyone's new toy; he was a sweet and easy baby, and people wanted to be with him. I was with him during the day, and went to sleep at Craig's at night.

Rex spent two or three nights a week with Jes; he may have still been a kid himself, but he wanted this child and was not at all happy I'd wanted to get a divorce. But I thought—I *knew*— Jes was better off with Rex or my mom than Craig and me. Craig didn't really want to be a father, so even if I was addicted to him, my rational self knew in the long run this relationship was a bad idea (not that I wouldn't have some even worse ideas later . . .). Craig and I couldn't even agree on how to raise a puppy, never mind a child. It was better Jes didn't become attached to him. I knew our relationship wouldn't last forever.

For the next few years, I alternated between living with Mom and Jes and living with Craig, and doing whatever job I managed not to quit. Life didn't have an interesting trajectory, but I had my son and my boyfriend and my weed and my beer, and I was okay. When Jes was old enough to go to school, I decided I'd join him, sort of, by going back to college to become a legal secretary. I wasn't particularly interested in being a secretary, but I felt that between being raised by a criminal defense attorney and being immersed in the details of my own legal case since the time of Polanski's arrest, I was practically a lawyer myself.

I was itching for change, and 1985 and 1986 gave me plenty to want to change from. First, life off and on with Craig was becoming increasingly insane. And then Nana, who had come to live with us a few years earlier, was often off her meds. For Mom, bringing anyone to visit was dicey. Nana would sit there, smoking and drinking her Chablis, flirting with Bob's friends. That behavior might be adorable when it's a snappy Betty White in an episode of *Hot in Cleveland,* but Mom found it cringe-inducing in real life. She was impossible to live with. Mom finally moved her to an apartment a few blocks away, but she'd still come to hang out every day. Her mind became more and more detached from the rest of her until it abandoned her entirely, and I came home to find her body lying on my bedroom floor. By the time I got home, the ambulance, recognizing she could not be resuscitated, had already left, and Mom was kneeling next to her, and had started chanting "Om Mani Padme Hum," urging her to Go Toward The Light. I think she was pretty much *at* the light at that point, so I told Mom I thought she could stop now. It was not a good moment. The paramedics had declared Nana dead and called for the coroner, and we had to wait over four hours. I was like, "How busy is the coroner? Did the entire population of Woodland Hills keel over today?" I'd never seen a dead person before. Nana was only sixty-two. Forty years of sedation and psychotropic drugs had taken their toll. But this woman had been an anchor in my life, always at the house to help with Jes, berating Craig if he treated me badly. I loved her. Mom was in shock for days. I learned soon what it was like to pick out a casket, trudge through a muddy cemetery in the pouring rain—things my mother could barely bring herself to do. This was the first time I ever had to care for my mother—which is not a bad thing to learn how to do.

There was something about the boring legal secretary school, the dead-end relationship, and the death of the crazy woman who, nevertheless, cared for me throughout my childhood, that combined to make me ever more volatile and self-destructive. After a few drinks, Craig and I would start in on each other, and I found it increasingly difficult to make up later. Some nights would end up with black eyes or broken glass. I have to say, I was always the one who threw the first punch.

When we finally broke up for good, it was not exactly amicable. He chucked a box of my stuff into my front yard. I was happy to see my rifle, but he kept our motorcycle and our dog, the only things I really cared about. It's not like I didn't get *anything* out of the relationship—because of Craig and the number of holes we both put in the wall, I got very good at spackling.

One of my friends, Vikki, was paying her way through our legal secretarial school with nude modeling—and with my I'll-try-anything-once mentality at the time, when a photographer said he thought my pictures would sell to *Penthouse,* I was happy to oblige. I think it is safe to say they ended up in a magazine that made *Penthouse* look like the *New York Review of Books.* I gave it my all, wearing a smile and little else.

On the one hand, it was kind of stupid. On the other . . . well, having now just celebrated my fiftieth birthday, I'm rather glad I have photos of my hot twenty-two-year-old self. Every woman should. (Though admittedly, every woman shouldn't sell them to a magazine.) I didn't even want the money; mostly I was looking for adventure. But perhaps there was some small part of my brain that enjoyed reclaiming what was mine. If a guy was going to use me to get off—as Polanski did all those years ago—well, at least now I'd be making the decision, and getting something out of it, too.

At that time I was in the middle of a romance that made me and Craig look like Ozzie and Harriet. Kyle was a handsome younger guy who swore we were meant to be together. He had been in some trouble before and by the time we started dating he had secretly started back down that road to drugs and crime. We loved each other madly, but that wasn't enough to save him. He was using and stealing and people were noticing.

Even my mother—not the single most observant person in the world—began to notice things went missing when he visited me. Inevitably, he ended up in jail. A normal person at that point might have been relieved. But no: In my delusional state, I took this as a sign that though friends and society wanted to keep us apart, we were meant to be together. It was us against the world. I just knew our situation was entirely unique in the history of modern civilization. So I married him—in the court house, before he was sentenced to some time in prison. All of us prison brides, we're all playing that song in our heads from "Leader of the Pack": "They all thought he was bad / But I knew he was sad . . ."

Because carrying on the way I was necessitated time away from my mother, I'd been spending a lot of time with Vikki. She had a next-door neighbor named Dave. The story he tells is that he saw a photo of me at Vikki's house; we were posing next to our dirt bikes and toting guns, dressed in cowboy boots and bikinis. Reportedly Dave saw the photo, pointed to me, and said, "I'm going to marry that girl." Vikki just laughed.

And she had good reason. At the time Dave was a twenty-year-old carpenter as well as a drum roadie for an old friend of mine who also lived in the apartment building. He was a professional horndog, with multiple girlfriends; he was spending his nights in Hollywood at the Rainbow, and he looked the part: parachute pants, bandanas on his legs, puka shell neck-lace with a "69" pendant. He pursued me relentlessly. Once he followed me into the bathroom to plead his case—while an "ex" and a none-too-pleased current girlfriend were sitting in the living room. But somehow it was more funny than obnox-ious. We became friends.

Soon I was seeing Dave, too—a sort of a friend-with-benefits situation (not uncommon for women with husbands on the in-side). But I couldn't take him seriously; Dave had such a crazy history. However, Dave had declared his love and was trying to prove it to me by being as devoted as a German shepherd. One day we were sitting in his car talking and I mentioned Kyle for about the four hundredth time and Dave said, "You know what your problem is? You're too proud to admit you're wrong." He was right. I was making an ass of myself. It was my special tal-ent. By this time, Kyle and I knew it was over. So we ended it. We were both tired.

Or so I thought. Apparently I hadn't had my fill of drama yet. While all this was going on, my mother, who had separated from Bob and started selling real estate in California, began talking about taking her earnings and finding a place to live on the Hawaiian island of Kauai—a place for all of us. It was, I believed, a pipe dream, and I had no intention of moving at that time. But Rex thought I might, and that I'd take our son away with me. That started a custody negotiation.

It was with more than a little relief that I discovered I hadn't been legally married to Kyle in the first place. I learned this by accident at the time Rex served me with the custody papers. I had no intention of moving then, but once served with papers I characteristically got all "no one's going to tell me what to do" and served him back. While we were busily tearing into each other, I learned that the quickie divorce we'd gotten a few years back in the Dominican Republic wasn't recognized in the United States, that in fact Rex and I were still married. So we called a truce, worked out our differences—which included getting a real divorce—and I had the great good fortune of having my marriage to Kyle declared null and void. I was probably the only person in that California courthouse getting a divorce and annulment on the same day. Ah, romance!

But I wasn't quite done with my weakness for bad boys. Before I'd met Dave, he had been arrested for selling a dime bag of weed, and now he had to serve his sentence. The night before he went to the county jail that everyone called Camp Snoopy, we kissed in a way that I knew would make me remember him when he was gone. Dave served two months in jail— oddly, both Kyle and Dave were at Camp Snoopy at the same time. Kyle knew Dave, and hated him, since he began asking me out the minute Kyle was gone. Fortunately, Kyle had no idea Dave was there. Dave knew, but Dave was in minimum security and they never crossed paths.

Dave served two months of his three-month sentence and got out on his twenty-first birthday. We celebrated by going to a bar and getting him his first legal beer.

That going-away kiss and the homecoming beer turned

into something serious: after a Labor Day camping trip he moved in with us. Dave wanted a bigger family. Less than a year later, I got pregnant. Things seemed to be settling down. I was still a party girl to some degree, but a party girl with a job—as a secretary at a computer company—and a man I loved. It was early spring 1988.

One day someone called at work and asked to speak to Samantha. Since the receptionist where I worked was also named Samantha, there was some confusion. Wait, they wanted to speak to Samantha because of something having to do with Roman Polanski? Who? What?

But *I* wasn't confused. I knew that ten years after Polanski was out of my life forever, he was back.

The next thing I knew, there was a photo of me in the feisty British tabloid the *Sunday Mirror,* under the headline STAY AWAY, POLANSKI. Photographers must have been hiding right outside my office. Never mind that the entire "interview" was made up; what really upset me was that it was another long "Sex Victim Girl" story, and one that said specifically where I worked and what kind of car I drove and even mentioned that I had a boyfriend.

And worse than that: I had never told Dave. I told him now—and had to explain. Being three years younger than I was, he was only ten when the story was all over the news. He'd heard of it, but it wasn't a big deal in his world. Until now. When he wasn't trying to charm a cute girl, Dave was a man of few words. He said little, but I knew he felt a great deal.

The story said:

Sex scandal girl Samantha Gailey has blocked hopes of a return to America for exiled film director Roman Polanski. The controversial film director fled to Paris 11 years ago to escape justice for having under-age sex with the young beauty.

Samantha, shown right in an exclusive Sunday Mirror *picture, will never let him forget the drunken, drug-crazed sex session he inflicted on her when she was just 13 years old.*

And despite a recent campaign waged by Polanski's Hollywood superstar friends to bring him back, the long-limbed blonde still says no.

"He's not coming back," said Samantha. "Over my dead body. This is my town, not his, and there is no way he is coming home. . . ."

The paper completely fabricated a quote from Larry: "We will oppose his return as long as I live. Can you imagine growing up with what she has had to grow up with?" And then, it concluded: ". . . Samantha still lives with her mother, trying to free herself from the long shadow cast over her by the sordid affair."

To my surprise, the picture taken of me was quite lovely, but the text told another story. In this piece I was bitter and resentful, an emotional cripple who still lived with my mother. For good measure the other photo in the article was a lingerie shot of Emmanuelle Seigner, the then twenty-one-year-old French model/actress of unsurpassable beauty whom Polanski was due to marry. The article suggested that Polanski thought it was time to "forgive and forget," and that a new marriage would pave the way for his return to the United States—as if marriage covered rape like paper covering rock.

It was a slap to him and his fiancée, in a way, the idea that he was marrying for PR purposes. Worse to me, however, was the idea that somehow my life was defined by my experience with Polanski. And this was as I felt my life coming together for maybe the first time. I was furious. I was just getting back on my feet; life as I imagined it was just beginning. And again the invasion of privacy, the vomiting up of all the awful memories.

I decided to call Larry. Surely there was something he could do.

But shortly after the tabloid published the story, two things happened that made me shelve my anger for a little while. First, I discovered that I was pregnant. And then, my mother, who actually *had* bought a place in Kauai, officially invited us to move with her—and we'd get six months' free rent.

There was nothing really holding us in California, and for Dave, who was from Van Nuys, moving to Kauai was a dream. I was nervous, but how could I say no? We had no idea what to expect and thought we were moving to the middle of the jungle (which, it turns out, we did, albeit one with a 7-Eleven and a few other stores).

I had been wavering about making such a radical move, but this article clinched it. I would never get away from reminders of what had happened if I stayed in Woodland Hills. It wasn't just the pervasiveness of physical reminders—the old party-ing pals who knew my story; the suburban tract house where I'd arrived that night, strung-out and spent; the homes and hills and bars where I'd tried to lose myself. It was Los Ange-les itself. There was something about being in a culture where attention-seeking is the norm, where the desire for fame is in the thoughts and aspirations and *sweat* of just about everyone you meet, that always made me flash back to Polanski.

It was time to take Dave, Jes, and my pregnant self and start over in the beautiful anonymity of Hawaii.

In October 1988 I moved to Kauai, the oldest of the Hawai-ian islands and arguably the most beautiful. Over the years dozens of movies, from *South Pacific* to *Jurassic Park* to *The Descendants,* have been filmed there. When I moved there in 1988 it was an unspoiled almost-wilderness, though in more recent years it has become a retreat and sometime second home for many people in the entertainment industry. (That celebrity-friendly vibe is meant to be part of its charm, but not to me; I am still suspicious and uncomfortable around people in the entertainment industry.) But if today it is the kind of place where people like Bette Midler and Sylvester Stallone can go grocery shopping undisturbed, back then it was also the kind of place where *I* could go undisturbed. Kauai is also a haven for people who want to get off the grid— the perfect, gorgeous country setting where you can have one or two little secrets and nobody knows—or if they know, they don't care. There is also, as I was soon to learn, a small-town mentality of "we take care of our own." There are the locals, and there is everyone else. If you live there, your neighbors have your back.

Dave and I got married in December 1989, when our son Alex was almost one. I was twenty-six; Dave was twenty-three. I was busy with my two sons, and Dave was finding a variety of jobs in this strange new world. We were happy.

There is also something about island life that seems to slow down time and encourage reflection. With the space to think, I realized that in my life of "look away," there was one thing I'd avoided above all else. I'm not a vindictive person by any means. I am still friendly with ex-lovers and ex-husbands; I am deeply grateful to and loyal to old friends, and I don't dwell on past fights or insults. (In fact, I have the very good fortune to have a lousy memory for that stuff.) I knew that Roman had written an autobiography. I was in it. And my family. And I had heard it wasn't flattering, to put it mildly. I didn't even want to buy it, so I finally asked Larry to send me the part of the book that pertained to me. I read it.

It's important to understand this. Back in 1978, after we requested that the most serious charges against Polanski be dropped, my family and I were harshly criticized: Did those people only report his crimes so they could get money through a civil suit? Larry had to state over and over again that there would not be a civil suit. After all, he said, the goal was to protect my anonymity, and a lawsuit would destroy that. So I'd always thought back on that criticism, and always thought that

I would not give anyone the satisfaction of thinking that the reporting of the rape was a play for money down the road.

But then, years after Polanski had published his autobiography—and after several other biographies of Polanski had come out, more or less restating his perspective of March 10, 1977—I'd had enough. Whatever hesitation I'd had over the years was gone.

Let me be clear: Much of what was said in Polanski's book was true. But there were also several terrible lies about me and my family—about my mother being flirtatious, about there being an unspoken erotic frisson between me and Roman, and so forth. You can call them *misperceptions* all you like; they're still lies and they hurt. With his autobiography, he was profiting from his misadventures and attempting to rationalize his crimes; there was a certain level of swagger and arrogance in it all. I decided to take control of a situation that had been out of my control for a long time. Still smarting from my appearance in that tabloid and having now read what Roman had put into print about me and my family, I decided to sue him for sexual assault in civil court.

My decision to sue was not impulsive and did not come easily. I knew that no matter how blameless I was, I risked looking greedy. Did something bad happen to you? Make some money! It's the American way! Also, the civil law system can be just as byzantine and arbitrary as the criminal one. There are no guarantees of fairness there, either. But it was starting to seem that it was the only chance of getting Polanski's voice muted. The suit was my way of saying, "Roman, shut up."

Don't get me wrong: the money was a factor as well. It was not just a way to punish Polanski; it was also a way of compensating me. I had two children (and would soon have one more), and neither Dave nor I made a great deal of money. I had no resources to sue magazines and newspapers when they printed lies about me, often lies that came from Polanski's autobiography. It seemed like they would never stop coming after me. And it seemed that everyone, including Roman, had profited from my assault—everyone except me. When tabloids offered me money for interviews in the past (the *National Enquirer* offered fifteen thousand dollars in 1977), I'd turned them down. This didn't make me noble; in fact, it might have made me naïve. But it was my version of integrity. Nobody else seemed to have the same scruples.

More important, when coming to this decision, I'd had a lot of dark years. Who knows if I would ever have been successful, but my ability to pursue the career I wanted was quashed before I had a chance to find out. There were long periods when the very effort of not dwelling on what had happened to me, of trying to ignore everything that was said about me in newspapers and on television, made me find some pretty stupid ways to numb myself. I take responsibility for my weaknesses and my bad decisions, but I also believe that my opportunities were reduced, and my life compromised, as a result of Polanski's rape of the thirteen-year-old me.

In most cases, this lawsuit would have been impossible—the statute of limitations for filing a civil suit in California would have run out years ago. But even though more than a decade had passed, I could still sue. Why? Two reasons. First, in California, the clock is not ticking until the child victim of a sexual assault case turns eighteen. Second, the statute of limitations isn't applicable during the period a defendant is out of the state. So because Polanski had left the country in February 1978 and stayed out, it was as if I were bringing this lawsuit in 1978, not 1989.

Polanski's lawyers had a job to do: they had to prove that whatever emotional distress I had in my life was not the fault of Polanski. So they would bring up the crazy Nana, the drug-addled friends, even the fact that I smoked marijuana with my sister when I was sixteen. And there was the suggestion that I had been molested as a child, which was what motivated me to accuse Polanski later on. Polanski's new lawyer, David Finkle, mentioned that I'd been asked by the district attorney whether I'd had sex with Bob, my mother's boyfriend—and wondered why I had been asked that question. "Try insensitivity," Larry shot back.

For the lawsuit I was deposed for days, as were members of my family. It was embarrassing to admit I had lied to the grand jury initially about both my sexual and drug experiences. I had said I had slept with someone twice before, when in fact it was once, and I had also lied about taking a Quaalude before meeting Polanski. I said I had when I hadn't. Why?

When Polanski was trying to persuade me to take the pill, I'd wanted him to think that when I said no I was speaking from experience—kind of "been there, done that, don't need to do it again." But once I'd lied to him, I felt I had to maintain that lie for the grand jury. As I said in this deposition: "I was afraid he would call me a liar, and people would further have no belief that what I was saying was true."

It was upsetting to hear the way my sister, Kim, thought my life had changed since Polanski. She described me as an introvert, a person who only went out when she had to and rarely socialized outside the home. Was she exaggerating? She certainly didn't think so.

And here's the thing. Maybe some of Polanski's lawyers' insinuations were valid. Who knows? They attacked my character, and their suggestion seemed to be that Polanski's raping me fit seamlessly into my already messy life. So really, what was the big deal? But that's sort of like arguing, "Your Honor, having her legs run over by a Mack truck doesn't change anything; she already had a limp."

The lawsuit dragged on over the next few years. (The press didn't find out about it until years later, because Larry had rather cleverly filed the suit under the title "Jane Doe v. R. Rpolanski." Making a typo meant that the case was indexed under the defendant's last name, which began with an *R*. So anyone looking for a case with the name Polanski wouldn't find it. (Remember, this was pre-Google.) During that time, I continued to have people show up at my house, photographing me and my family, trying to convince me it would be "good for me" to tell my story.

Two in particular stand out. First, there were the women I called the Weird Book Ladies. One day, two women showed

200 | SAMANTHA GEIMER

up at my house saying they were looking for my mother; they had some gifts for her. I assumed they were real estate clients. With my baby Alex on my hip, I walked them into her house so we could put the packages they had on her table. Once back outside, they admitted they were really looking for me. I felt so stupid, so violated, like I'd walked a burglar right into our home. They had written a book called *Perfect Victim: The True Story of "The Girl in the Box"*—about a girl who'd been kept in a coffin as a sex slave for seven years. And—good news—for their next project they wanted to write *my* story. The idea that they associated my story with this other one was disturbing enough; even worse was the letter they wrote me a few weeks later, offering to pay one hundred thousand dollars if I cooperated. And if I didn't? "Eventually someone will do the story anyway, and once again, Sam will be left with nothing." The veiled threats weren't lost on me, and I refused to have anything to do with them. But even after I told them to talk to my lawyer, they continued to send presents—a crystal lighthouse, some potpourri—even some Mickey Mouse toys for the kids. (All of which I gave away. It was sad; we needed money and my children would have enjoyed those presents, but it just felt wrong.) All I can say is this: When a person's opening conversational salvo is "We don't mean to frighten you" (as theirs was), prepare to be really, really frightened. I know I was.

Then in 1990 a guy from the tabloid television news show *A Current Affair* parked his van across the street from my house for three days with a video camera shooting out of a tinted window toward my house. He refused to leave. He had three huge flower arrangements delivered, one each for Mom, Kim, and me. He also tried to make me an offer I couldn't refuse. He'd pay me five thousand dollars to talk, and if I didn't, he'd just do the story without me. It took us two days to notice the camera, and during that time my children, friends, and family had all been filmed. I was trapped in my own house, sitting on the floor, because he had a camera pointed at us and I didn't want to be photographed. This lasted for several days, until Larry got hold of the right person at the show and gave him a lesson on the legal meaning of extortion.

This kind of attention was more than just a nuisance. I lived with my husband, mom, and little kids on this remote island, and it had been so easy to find me; and because I wasn't naturally on guard, I'd let these unpleasant, slightly menacing strangers into my home. It made me feel so stupid and vulnerable. How could I protect my family from this kind of thing? I couldn't.

The most revealing incident from those years occurred when Larry went to Paris to depose Polanski himself. It was a fairly routine proceeding that took place in a lawyer's office. There was a court reporter Larry had brought from the United States, Polanski's lawyer David Finkle, and Polanski himself. After two hours there was a break for lunch. Larry went to eat by himself in a café close to the office, not noticing until later that Polanski and his lawyer were at a nearby table.

In order to leave the restaurant, Larry had to pass by Polanski's table. This was, needless to say, a bit uncomfortable.

As he was going by, Polanski motioned for him to stop: "Larry, Larry, come over." Then Polanski said to him, matter-of-factly, "If you had seen her naked, she was so beautiful, you would have wanted to fuck her, too."

Polanski never denied saying that. But he was livid with Larry for relating the incident to Roger Gunson over a casual lunch. Gunson reported the incident in a signed statement to the DA's office. Ironically, Polanski should have been very grateful to Larry. It was Larry who convinced the court to protect my rights and keep me from testifying, making it possible for him to get the plea bargain. Without that, Polanski probably would have served at least a few years in jail.

The lawsuit began in 1988 and was settled five years later for a six-figure sum. Polanski, however, avoided paying it for years, finally forcing us to file a notice of default, which had the unfortunate side effect of putting the dollar amount in the public record. The other terms of our settlement, most of which have remained confidential, include that Roman was forbidden from ever discussing the events of that night, or ever speaking about my family or me. I agreed not to commercially exploit the story and to assist if I could in his efforts to resolve his legal issues with the United States.

I was grateful for the money when it eventually showed up. But it is hardly a sum that would compensate for helping Polanski get back into the country if I thought it were the wrong thing to do.

CHAPTER 15

For me, the 1990s were mostly about raising children. I had my third son, Matt, in 1993. I worked for a successful real estate developer on the island, and my husband, Dave, became, quite literally, a cowboy: He was the operations manager for the developer's three-hundred-plus acres of various vacation and rental properties, which included a cattle ranch. I found great joy in living in a small town, where you know your neighbors and their kids and everybody looks out for each other; it was different from living on the mainland. The kids could go down to the park to play or down to the river to fish and you didn't have to worry whether they were safe. Jes didn't even have to wear shoes to school for the first year or two we were there. Alex was free to walk to school and go to the park and beach with his pack of buddies in complete safety. Matty was in the ocean learning to spearfish when he was seven. Doors unlocked, windows open, fresh air, afternoons at the beach fishing and barbecuing. Nice. We were a haven for dogs (five or six at a time, usually; my mother has six mastiffs) and peo-ple; it would be very strange *not* to have friends, or the kids of friends, living with us. I even remember Hurricane Iniki in 1992, which flattened the entire island—no phone, TV, or power for three months—as a pretty happy time. It's not as bad as you think, being disconnected from the grid when you are connected to other creatures in so many other profound ways. When the electricity comes back, you're a little shocked to real-ize you didn't miss much.

There was one great sadness during that time, however. In 1995, my father died. Jack Gailey and I hadn't seen each other and rarely had spoken in years. He had another family; I lived in Hawaii and hadn't been back to York for a long, long time. He'd been in declining health, and when I heard he'd taken a bad turn, I got on a plane to see him. I didn't make it in time. The last thing I'd said to him on the phone was "I love you, Daddy. I'm coming to see you." The next time I saw him, he was in a ceramic urn at his funeral.

The wake was in Dad's home. Everyone was lovely and wel-coming. Dave needed something to do so he found all the tools and worked to clean up the large yard where the services would be held. I had some time alone, so I wandered in and out of those familiar and formidable rooms I'd grown up in. I loved that house. It was still a little spooky, but at the same time I felt like it knew I was back. That house to me was somehow like a living thing, a childhood friend. It welcomed me, too.

I found myself sitting at my father's desk. I felt I'd been a favorite of my father's as a child, but I also felt I was a disappointment: no college education, wild drug past, pregnant at eighteen, married at nineteen. As I sat at the desk, I was startled by something: an eight-by-ten photo of me on his shelf. He hadn't forgotten me. I was still loved. Why hadn't we spoken more over the years? What happened after Polanski that made me feel, more and more, that I wasn't his little girl?

. . .

My easygoing life on Kauai helped me continue my life of "look away," albeit more productively and happily than I did in my twenties. It was easy to turn away from the past, even when Roman Polanski, through his attorneys, would intermittently try to work out a deal with the DA so he could return to this country. Far from California, tucked away in paradise, my friends and neighbors in Kauai couldn't care less about Roman Polanski or his films or what happened to me. Sometimes the stories of his efforts to return were just rumors; sometimes they were true:

By Steve James

Thursday, October 2, 1997

LOS ANGELES (Reuters): Hollywood was abuzz Tuesday over reports that fugitive director Roman Polanski might return from Europe to face sentencing in the teenage sex scandal that scuttled his US film career and sent him into a 20 year exile.

Several local TV stations reported the Polish-born maker of such classic films as "Rosemary's Baby" and "Chinatown" was ready to come back to Los Angeles to be punished for having sex with a 13-year-old girl.

They said Polanski, now 64, had reached an agreement with the Los Angeles district attorney's office that if he returns from France he would not serve time in jail.

The district attorney's office denied any deals had been made.

Court records cited by the local reports showed Polanski's lawyer Douglas Dalton had met twice in the last year with Deputy District Attorney Roger Gunson and Los Angeles Superior Court Judge Larry Fidler.

A source in the prosecutor's office acknowledged there had been sporadic contact during the years with Polanski's lawyer over the director's attempt to work out a way he could return to the United States.

But officially, the district attorney's office said its position had not changed in the last 20 years.

"Mr. Polanski must surrender," said a spokeswoman. "We have not agreed to any sentence."

This particular negotiation may have actually worked, if it weren't for one snafu. The judge involved, Larry Paul Fidler (who also presided over the Phil Spector murder trial ten years later), reportedly insisted the Polanski proceedings be televised. A court spokesman later called this supposed demand "a complete fabrication."

I don't know which story is true, but I do know the deal fell through.

. . .

The media had an insatiable appetite for Polanski stories, and every time there was a rumor of a possible return, it would be covered—and I would be dragged along into it. Though I had no power to influence what was a legal matter, it didn't matter to the writers and editors whose main focus was on word counts and sensationalism. In the rush toward a fat paycheck, I didn't always come out so well. The *Vanity Fair* story published in April 1997 is a good example. *Vanity Fair* dines out on celebrity and crime, so this subject was, of course, irresistible.

Author Jill Robinson, who grew up in Hollywood and whose father, Dore Schary, once ran MGM, published an article in *Vanity Fair* under the slug "The Exile" and titled "Polanski's Inferno." She had, shall we say, a whimsical approach to facts. Beginning with a phone interview with Polanski where he noted that he lived through a time where "we were doing everything," the article goes on to say that the Sharon Tate murders had so damaged Polanski that some sort of incident seemed almost inevitable. Describing Polanski as the kind of man who "seduced the magic out of you," Robinson then insinuates that I would only talk to her if I were paid off with a trip to Disneyland (in fact she wanted to meet face-to-face, and thought I should fly to Los Angeles on my own dime to do just that). She then said I was prickly because her story wasn't just about me (oh yes, the person who had been retaining a lawyer to keep herself *out* of the media), and I was bitter about the rape and its aftermath because I hadn't succeeded in Hollywood. "She reminds me of the Unsinkable Molly Brown, still longing, in her way, to be 'Up where the people are.'" I thought at the time: Perhaps she was confusing me with herself.

I wrote to the magazine, enumerating some of the fabrications—that my mother did not sleep with Polanski, I did not have a "love bite" on my neck when Polanski met me, Polanski did not choose my clothes while I stood there in panties and bra—and of course, the fact that I was not exchanging trips to Disneyland for access. The Molly Brown allusion is the most baffling. If I, like Molly Brown, were a relentless social climber, I must have been the worst social climber in history, leaving Los Angeles to live quietly and happily and anonymously on a remote island.

I was not the only one to take exception to this piece. Polanski weighed in—objecting, among other things, to being called an "exile" from the United States when in fact he is and always was a French citizen. And Anjelica Huston's note rather hilariously and succinctly sums up how much the author had gone off the rails. "I would like to set the record straight. At no point have I ever described Roman Polanski as a freak, nor have I ever seen him in the nude."

Vanity Fair issued a snotty non-apology: "We apologize for any possible misunderstanding, but have no reason to believe that one did occur."

(Several years later, Polanski sued and won an $84,000 judgment against *Vanity Fair* for a 2002 article on Elaine's restaurant where the writer claimed that Polanski had stopped by the watering hole and tried to pick up a hot blonde on the way to his wife's funeral. Polanski was nowhere near the restaurant at the time. Oops!)

The most upsetting part of the story wasn't the lies. It was the version of the truth they dredged up and published—the intimate sexual questions and answers from the original grand jury testimony when I was thirteen years old. Good work, Robinson. Nice move, *Vanity Fair.* Bet it sold a lot of magazines.

· · ·

By the late 1990s I had finally decided to come out of hiding: I did an interview with *Inside Edition* where I revealed my identity. This was a relief, even if it did cause a flood of ancillary articles—particularly whenever Polanski, who now had a beautiful young wife, two little children and a flourishing film career in Europe, attempted again to broker a return to the United States without being arrested and thrown in jail. But I was tired of hiding and being afraid, tired of people making up lies about me. So I figured I'd say here I am. If you have a question, ask it. If you have something to say, don't think I won't say something back.

The whole issue flared in 2003 when Polanski was nominated for an Academy Award for Best Director for his 2002 film, *The Pianist.* This partly autobiographical movie about a Polish-Jewish musician struggling to survive the destruction of the Warsaw Ghetto during World War II was by all accounts extraordinary (I haven't seen it; as you can imagine, I'm not exactly sitting around waiting for the next Polanski release). But there was, predictably, outrage in certain quarters that a child rapist and fugitive would be nominated for best direc- tor. Never mind the absurdity of asking me whether Polanski should win an Oscar for a movie I'd never seen; this time, with the onslaught of calls and instructions to my children not to answer the phone, there was a great deal of upset for my chil- dren: *Oh, something bad happened to Mom. Oh, now we're all a part of it. Mom is damaged.*

(The controversy had its own life, of course, but it might have been fueled by the not-dissimilar incident a few years earlier involving Woody Allen, who was found to be having an affair with the adopted daughter of his lover Mia Farrow. Mia Farrow then accused him of molesting the daughter they adopted together. He was vilified, but that didn't keep him from being nominated for six Academy Awards as a director and a screenwriter in the years following.)

The question is this: Should a man's personal life dictate the way we judge his work? I gave my own answer in an op-ed piece I wrote for the *Los Angeles Times* in February 2003, right before the Oscars. It was titled "Judge the Movie, Not the Man."

I met Roman Polanski in 1977, when I was 13 years old. I was in ninth grade that year, when he told my mother that he wanted to shoot pictures of me for a French magazine. That's what he said, but instead, after shooting pictures of me at Jack Nicholson's house on Mulholland Drive, he did something quite different. He gave me champagne and a piece of a Quaalude. And then he took advantage of me.

It was not consensual sex by any means. I said no, repeatedly, but he wouldn't take no for an answer. I was alone and I didn't know what to do. It was scary and, looking back, very creepy. Those may sound like kindergarten words, but that's the way it feels to me. It was a very long time ago, and it is hard to remember exactly the way everything happened. But I've had to repeat the story so many times, I know it by heart.

We pressed charges, and he pleaded guilty. A plea bargain was agreed to by his lawyer, my lawyer and the district attorney, and it was approved by the judge. But to our amazement, at the last minute the judge went back on his word and refused to honor the deal.

Worried that he was going to have to spend 50 years in prison—rather than just time already served—Mr. Polanski fled the country. He's never been back, and I haven't seen him or spoken to him since.

Looking back, there can be no question that he did something awful. It was a terrible thing to do to a young girl. But it was also 25 years ago—26 years next month. And, honestly, the publicity surrounding it was so traumatic that what he did to me seemed to pale in comparison.

Now that he's been nominated for an Academy Award, it's all being reopened. I'm being asked: Should he be given the award? Should he be rewarded for his behavior? Should he be allowed back into the United States after fleeing 25 years ago?

Here's the way I feel about it: I don't really have any hard feelings toward him, or any sympathy, either. He is a stranger to me.

But I believe that Mr. Polanski and his film should be honored according to the quality of the work. What he does for a living and how good he is at it have nothing to do with me or what he did to me. I don't think it would be fair to take past events into consideration. I think that the academy members should vote for the movies they feel deserve it. Not for people they feel are popular.

And should he come back? I have to imagine he would rather not be a fugitive and be able to travel freely. Personally, I would like to see that happen. He never should have been put in the position that led him to flee. He should have received a sentence of time served 25 years ago, just as we all agreed. At that time, my lawyer, Lawrence Silver, wrote to the judge that the plea agreement should be accepted and that that guilty plea would be sufficient contrition to satisfy us. I have not changed my mind.

I know there is a price to pay for running. But who wouldn't think about running when facing a 50-year sentence from a judge who was clearly more interested in his own reputation than a fair judgment or even the well-being of the victim?

If he could resolve his problems, I'd be happy. I hope that would mean I'd never have to talk about this again. Sometimes I feel like we both got a life sentence.

My attitude surprises many people. That's because they didn't go through it all; they don't know everything that I know. People don't understand that the judge went back on his word. They don't know how unfairly we were all treated by the press.

Talk about feeling violated! The media made that year a living hell, and I've been trying to put it behind me ever since.

Today, I am very happy with my life. I have three sons and a husband. I live in a beautiful place and I enjoy my work. What more could I ask for? No one needs to worry about me.

The one thing that bothers me is that what happened to me in 1977 continues to happen to girls every day, yet people are interested in me because Mr. Polanski is a celebrity. That just never seems right to me. It makes me feel guilty that this attention is directed at me, when there are certainly others out there who could really use it.

Editor's note: The Times' *usual practice is not to name victims of sexual crimes. Samantha Geimer's name is used here with her consent.*

That piece created a firestorm, and the day it was published, February 23, 2003, Larry Silver and I appeared on *Larry King Live* to discuss it. "What happened that day," Silver said, "both to Polanski and to some extent the American judicial system—I really think it was a shameful day."

A few weeks later, Polanski won the Oscar for Best Director. He could not come to Hollywood for the ceremony. I never thought Roman would win, and I was quietly thrilled for his victory. It felt like a little strike against political correctness. Let's take all of this out of the realm of what happened twenty-five years ago, and let's just really consider the man as an artist.

Marina Zenovich, a filmmaker who made documentaries on the eccentric French businessman/politician Bernard

Tapie (and would go on to make a film in 2013 about the co-median Richard Pryor called *Omit the Logic*) took note of Lar-ry's comments on the *Larry King* show—the idea that it was a shameful day for American justice. Marina is drawn to people who leave a trail of chaos in their wake, so Polanski was an excellent subject for her. Her documentary, *Roman Polanski: Wanted and Desired*, which Larry and I participated in, was the first accurate public accounting of the case. It aired on HBO in 2008. Initially I participated because I was scared not to: after the awful *Vanity Fair* story, I always tried to cooperate with the press, fearing they would make up terrible things if I didn't. When the movie premiered at the Sundance Film Festival in Utah it was a hit, and I was so happy for Marina—happy, too, that she had invited me to New York City for the HBO premiere. I figured that the chance to see a movie premiere in New York would be a once in a lifetime invitation, and I thought it was time for mom to come out of hiding too. We could revisit our time in New York City in 1976, before our lives changed forever.

Once I was actually at the party, I was uncomfortable, and hugged the wall; the thought that I was at this party with all those celebrities and other luminaries simply because I'd been raped by some old goat seemed kind of mortifying. But I wanted to support Marina and the film. The way she laid it out so perfectly finally gave us a way to understand it all. To see it from the outside, not within the craziness. It brought my mother closure and comfort—and that, to me, was an extraordinary gift.

Writing about the case and Zenovich's documentary for the *New Yorker* in December 2009, Jeffrey Toobin explained how fame can be a double-edged sword. "The force of celebrity had buffeted the case once more," Toobin wrote. "It had helped Polanski by persuading his victim to support a plea deal, and by inspiring a fawning probation report; it hurt him by drawing suspicion to his legitimate travel to Germany and prompting Rittenband's erratic decisions. Celebrity now helped by drawing Zenovich's attention which, in turn, led to new questions about the case against him. His lawyers decided to make yet another attempt to resolve it."

In December 2008, Polanski's legal team filed a motion in Los Angeles County Superior Court asking for dismissal of the Polanski case, on the grounds that in 1977 he'd been deprived of due process of law. Larry was present to demonstrate my family's support.

Chad Hummel, who'd been recruited to Polanski's legal team, argued that Polanski's sentence at the Chino psychiatric facility "was intended to be his entire sentence . . . so this notion that somehow there was a fleeing from the sentence is not true. . . ." He went on to accuse the judge and others of improprieties. "In our system, we simply cannot tolerate backroom communications between prosecutors and judges that influence a sentence and that cut out the defendant and his counsel from those communications. . . . That's at the heart of this request."

This attempt turned out to hoist Polanski on his own petard, leading to his arrest in Switzerland and the extradition proceedings. To the Los Angeles DA's office, this was like ripping a scab off a wound. "This case is about a 44-year-old defendant who plied a 13-year-old girl with drugs and alcohol, then against her consent, committed acts of oral copulation, sodomy and sexual intercourse upon her," the DA's office wrote. The more accurate statement would be: It's about a defendant who pled guilty to unlawful sexual intercourse with a minor. But that did not have the dramatic effect the DA's office needed, and I really felt the statement was intended to humiliate me, since I was not cooperating with their efforts. "Petitioner's flight, whatever his motivations, and his failure to take responsibility for his crimes is at the heart of the extraordinary delays in this case." While acknowledging there may have been wrongdoing back in 1977, the presiding judge, Peter Espinoza, dismissed the motion on the grounds of the "fugitive disentitlement doctrine." Which basically means, "Get your ass back here, and then we'll talk."

This latest foray by Polanski's legal team infuriated the DA's office, and heated up a cold case. Compounding this tactical error was the fact that this was an election year. Los Angeles DA Steve Cooley, already in his third term as district attorney, was running for attorney general. (He had noisily protested when his predecessor, Gil Garcetti, attempted to win a third term after saying he'd only serve two. Once in office, Cooley apparently decided that the city couldn't do without him.) Cooley, a Republican in a blue state, had become increasingly unpopular, and was already facing a great deal of controversy by saying he would uphold Proposition 8, the divisive California bill banning same-sex marriage. He needed to turn attention to an issue that everyone could agree on: getting tough on Polanski and making him return to face justice. A no-brainer, right? Think again.

On September 22, 2009, after finding out that Polanski would be traveling through Austria and Switzerland, Cooley sent out a series of emails researching which country had a better extradition record with the United States. They went with Switzerland, and on September 26, when he entered Switzerland en route to the Zurich Film Festival where he was to be honored, Polanski was arrested and incarcerated.

Then the silly season began. Events felt more like scenes from *Dumb and Dumber* than examples of our noble system at work. David Wells, the DA assigned to handle cases in Rittenband's courtroom (though not the Polanski case), had bragged in *Roman Polanski: Wanted and Desired* that he had lobbied Judge Rittenband to entice Polanski to come back from Germany, and then to give him a harsher sentence. While this may have made it seem that Wells played a more important part in the proceedings, he seemed to be admitting to an ethical breach that could have resulted in his disbarment. (A DA is prohibited from discussing sentencing with the judge, even if the case isn't his.) To everyone's surprise, Wells suddenly announced in an interview that his statements in the documentary film were not true.

"They interviewed me in the Malibu courthouse when I was still a DA, and I embellished the story," Wells said in an interview with the Associated Press. "I'm a guy who cuts to the chase—I lied. It embarrasses the hell out of me."

Why did he choose to admit to lying now? Well, he was retired, so presumably had nothing to lose. But surely there must have been pressure from his pals in the DA's office.

This judicial malfeasance was part of Polanski's case that the court was treating him improperly, even illegally. So when Wells claimed he had lied in the documentary about having acted unethically, he was in fact weakening Polanski's case for returning without additional punishment. That seemed to be the idea, anyway.

But the DA's office wasn't through with their propaganda. To strengthen their case, they needed Polanski to look not like a rapist, but a *serial* rapist. Enter television personality/attorney Gloria Allred. On May 14, 2010, she was on television (as usual), an attractive woman by her side. My initial thought was, "For goodness sakes, how many mistresses did Tiger Woods have?" But then I got a shock.

Allred's press conference was with Charlotte Lewis, a British starlet and *Playboy* model who'd had a small role in the Polanski production of *Pirates*. Lewis claimed that Polanski had sexually abused her "in the worst possible way" when she was underage in Paris. (She was sixteen at the time of the incident, which is legally not underage in France.) "He took advantage of me and I have lived with the effects of his behavior ever since it occurred," said Lewis, reading from a prepared statement at a news conference in Allred's office. "All I want is justice." Then Allred invited anyone else who'd been abused by Roman to contact her. Of course.

I had several thoughts. The first one was cautionary for Ms. Lewis. I know how this all works: someone convinced you that this was a great idea, that you needed to do it. But I know what comes next. This publicity will turn around and bite you. In a few weeks the press will be reporting terrible things about you. Nobody walks away from this unscathed. Gloria Allred and the DA are just using you, and you are probably going to be sorry you let them.

My second thought was toward the other "victims" Ms. Allred was inviting to step forward. I hoped there were none, but if people did step forth, all the questions and accusations would begin: this one wasn't underage, this one wasn't non-consensual . . . the press would be parsing everyone's morality and motives . . . and mine would be lumped together in the "questionable" pile.

And that, more or less, is what happened. Another woman interested in justice—Edith Vogelhut, a former model and magazine editor—came forward with the claim that in 1974, when she was twenty-one, Polanski handcuffed her at a party at Jack Nicholson's house and sodomized her repeatedly. "I kind of knew we were going to have sex," she said, but "did not expect to be sodomized."

"I see this naked Roman Polanski walking to me with these two brandies," she says, adding that they also smoked pot and that he gave her ecstasy before handcuffing her. "He grabs me by the hair, jerks my head up, snaps amyl nitrate under my nose, and enters me anally," says Vogelhut. "I hurt. This was rape."

You know what? I wasn't there; I don't know what happened. No one should be forced to have sex against their will, and everyone has the right to say no. But why wait so long to accuse Polanski, and then only with the glare of the spotlight on them?

I'm not making a judgment; Edith Vogelhut's experience sounds awful. But if she was so heinously abused in 1974, as an adult, where was she when I was being called a slut and a liar in 1977? Moreover, I couldn't help thinking at the time, Why would anyone want to be a part of this? (It was reported that she was trying to sell a book.)

And as for Charlotte, soon after her accusation, the retribution followed. It was reported that in a 1999 interview with the British tabloid *News of the World,* Charlotte Lewis had stated that she'd been Polanski's girlfriend for six months after the shooting of *Pirates,* adding, "I knew that Roman had done something bad in the United States, but I wanted to be his lover." Some media outlets found this pretty difficult to square with her earlier claims of sexual abuse.

Here's the thing: There are some experiences that are genuinely impossible to get past. At the same time this circus was going on, Amber Dubois's parents were weeping at the sentencing hearing for the man who had brutally murdered their daughter. Will they completely recover? I doubt it.

This is so different. We've all done something in our lives we regret, something that is stupid; or something awful and stupid is done to us. For 90 percent of these situations, there comes a time when you need to let it go—unless you don't want to. And then, in a sense, it's your problem.

Why was the State of California interested in spending time and resources to extradite Roman Polanski? Has the DA cleaned up all the drug and gang violence in California? No more problems with illegal immigration? Are they releasing thousands of criminals just to make room for him? Was it not obvious to everyone that the DA was doing this as a means of furthering his own career, with utter disrespect and disregard for the victim in this case? He is doing the opposite of his job.

Because of his fame, Polanski had been lied to and manipulated by our criminal justice system. This notoriety drew corrupt and venal people to him like moths to a flame, from the judge on down. Celebrity can be a benefit and a curse. There is massive privilege, but that privilege and attention can easily backfire on you, too, as we see almost daily. Maybe if Polanski had been a nobody he would still have gotten the case pleaded down, been sentenced to six months for unlawful sex with a minor, and served two or three months—exactly as he did. But he wasn't a nobody; he was somebody whose fame and power made everyone involved with the case worry about *themselves* in relation to it. Who would seem tough? Who would seem like a pushover? Who could use the case for professional or personal gain?

And here's the big issue: Who, exactly, would be served if Roman Polanski went to jail? True, this was a man who liked inappropriately young girls. Hell, he eventually married a remarkably young girl—Emmanuelle Seigner, who was only twenty-three when they wed in 1989 (he was fifty-six). But he was not a pedophile; he was not hanging around schoolyards. He was not violent, he was not rough; he was, mostly, a selfish, arrogant man—and one who was not even a complete outlier given his place and the cultural moment.

I was reminded of who Roman Polanski was in those days when I read Peter Biskind's seminal book on Hollywood from the late 1960s through the 1970s, *Easy Riders, Raging Bulls: How the Sex-Drugs-and-Rock 'n' Roll Generation Saved Hollywood*. Peter Bart, the Paramount producer who worked with Polanski on *Rosemary's Baby,* called him "a brilliant man, the best read, most cultured director I have ever met in my life. But . . . he was always at the edge of the flame." Life was not making sense to him. He went for the pleasures that were a sure thing. One of those pleasures was young girls. Robert Towne, *Chinatown* screenwriter, talked about rewriting the script with Polanski at a hotel, and how they would fight "over the teenyboppers that Roman would

run out and take Polaroid pictures of diving off the fucking diving board without tops on. Which was distracting."

Over and over I've been called a Polanski apologist, with
the implication that I have been manipulated into taking his
side by nefarious people in positions of power. I am not apolo-
gizing for him and I didn't think his art somehow makes up
for what he did. (Full disclosure: I don't even like his movies.)
Mostly what I am is a person with common sense and a belief
that motive does play a role in judging a crime. Roman Polanski was a man who was horny and high on March 10, 1977.
That's it. I do not think his motive was to hurt me, even if, un-
avoidably, he did. I consider the integrity of our justice system
far more important than the punishment of one man, for one
crime, even if I was the victim.

Those were my thoughts. And while many disagreed with
me, Polanski's arrest and attempted extradition from Switzerland proved to be red meat for pundits and pontificators on
both sides of the Atlantic.

For those who worshipped him as an artist . . . well, if Polanski
wasn't already revered enough in France, this arrest and attempt
at extradition made him into a martyr. First, the Société des Au-
teurs et Compositeurs Dramatiques circulated a petition signed
by more than one hundred people in the film industry, including Martin Scorsese, Pedro Almodóvar, and Woody Allen:

We have learned the astonishing news of Roman Polanski's ar-
rest by the Swiss police on September 26th, upon arrival in Zurich

(Switzerland) while on his way to a film festival where he was due to receive an award for his career in filmmaking.

His arrest follows an American arrest warrant dating from 1978 against the filmmaker, in a case of morals.

Filmmakers in France, in Europe, in the United States and around the world are dismayed by this decision. It seems inadmissible to them that an international cultural event, paying homage to one of the greatest contemporary filmmakers, is used by the police to apprehend him.

By their extraterritorial nature, film festivals the world over have always permitted works to be shown and for filmmakers to present them freely and safely, even when certain States opposed this.

The arrest of Roman Polanski in a neutral country, where he assumed he could travel without hindrance, undermines this tradition: it opens the way for actions of which no one can know the effects.

Roman Polanski is a French citizen, a renowned and international artist now facing extradition. This extradition, if it takes place, will be heavy in consequences and will take away his freedom.

Filmmakers, actors, producers and technicians—everyone involved in international filmmaking—want him to know that he has their support and friendship.

On September 16th, 2009, Mr. Charles Rivkin, the US Ambassador to France, received French artists and intellectuals at the embassy. He presented to them the new Minister Counselor for Public Affairs at the embassy, Ms. Judith Baroody. In perfect French she lauded the Franco-American friendship and recommended the development of cultural relations between our two countries.

If only in the name of this friendship between our two countries,
we demand the immediate release of Roman Polanski.

Two things stand out to me in this petition. One, that the
only reference to Polanski's crime is that it was "a case of morals." A case of morals? Really? Then this important and self-
important document stops to pay tribute to the American
minister's "perfect French." If Polanski had raped me in perfect French, all this subsequent unpleasantness could have
been avoided. *Vive la France!*

Bernard-Henri Lévy, the French writer and philosopher,
started his own petition of famous well-wishers—everyone
from Salman Rushdie and Jean-Luc Godard to Diane Von
Furstenberg. The arrest was called a "judicial lynching" by a
society of Polish filmmakers. Swiss editorial pages did a lot of
breast-beating about how a "trap" had been laid for the director in their country. The French and Polish foreign ministers
took their complaint to then secretary of state Hillary Clin-
ton, and in an interview with a French radio state, Bernard
Kouchner, the French foreign minister, said "This affair is
frankly a bit sinister." And Frédéric Mitterrand, the French
culture minister, called the arrest "callous" and "absolutely
horrifying." (He had to back down a little after people remem-
bered his 2005 memoir, where he'd written about his own pas-
sion for underage young boys he'd pay for sex while traveling in
Thailand. *Vive la France encore!*)

There was equally strong reaction from those who wanted

Polanski returned to the United States and were disgusted by the support he got from the intellectual elite. Katha Pollitt wrote an impassioned and widely read piece in the *Nation*.

> *It's enraging that literary superstars who go on and on about human dignity, and human rights, and even women's rights (at least when the women are Muslim) either don't see what Polanski did as rape, or don't care, because he is, after all, Polanski— an artist like themselves. That some of his defenders are women is particularly disappointing. Don't they see how they are signing on to arguments that blame the victim, minimize rape, and bend over backwards to exonerate the perpetrator? Error of youth, might have mistaken her age, teen slut, stage mother—is that what we want people to think when middle-aged men prey on ninth-graders?*

The observations weren't all heavy stuff. In fact, while I recoiled from the serious commentary—hearing the details of the case repeated and exaggerated ad nauseam—I rather enjoyed the jokes, even when I was the butt of them. The funniest riff came from Chris Rock on Jay Leno's show. "People are defending Roman Polanski because he made some good movies? Are you kidding me? He made good movies thirty years ago, Jay! Even Johnnie Cochran don't have the nerve to go, 'Well, did you see O. J. play against New England?'"

. . .

Throughout all this, I tried to keep my head down and stay away from all the press idiocy. It wasn't always easy. For one thing, as I noted earlier, there were cameras set up outside my house. And not just cameras. My son Alex remembers reporters coming over to him and saying, "Listen, we'll give you money to make a statement. Here's twenty bucks if you just say, 'No comment.'" At one point my sons started taking pictures of *them*. Once—that fateful day in September 2009, after Roman's arrest—I gave photographers the finger. You don't flip off paparazzi. But it was like my hand was possessed. I'm looking at my upright third digit going, *You betrayed me, you York, Pennsylvania, fuck-you hand.*

It was amazing what the press would do to try to get me to make news. One of the British tabloids called Larry and said they were willing to pay me "real money" for an interview: $75,000, $80,000. For me, that was more than a year's salary, for one hour of my time. I needed the money. My *kids* needed the money. I thought to myself, If I can be paid to say what I've been trying to get across all this time, that would be great.

The tabloid writer called and called. Larry, as my attorney and spokesman, told him I was willing. Then this: "I just spoke to my editor in England," the writer said to Larry. "If we're paying that amount of money, she has to say she's withdrawn her forgiveness for Polanski."

First, I never used the word *forgive* publicly—what I did in my heart was a private matter. More important, while I struggled to understand and get past what happened, I was never so arrogant to suggest that I had the power to grant "forgiveness." Forgiveness was for my peace of mind; it had little to do with him.

Gee, thanks but no thanks.

During the weeks and months after Polanski's arrest in Switzerland, I once again felt joined to this man who was almost a stranger: in a sense, both Polanski and I were being held against our wills. It was hard not to think about him in jail. I would wake up in the morning free to do as I liked, while he was locked in a cell. I thought this is just all so wrong. I was actually relieved when he was released to "house arrest" in the chalet he owned in Switzerland.

While Larry worked behind the scenes to free me from this hell by bringing closure (which meant enabling Polanski to come back to the States without the threat of further incarceration), I had the pleasure of watching myself being excoriated in the press. Here was the problem: I wasn't being a good victim. A good victim asks for help and cries on TV and parades around telling her story of woe for public consumption. We are told we are "helping others" by exposing ourselves in that way. The public appetite for other people's misery demands it.

And I just wasn't cooperating.

Jaclyn Friedman, editor of *Yes Means Yes! Visions of Female Sexual Power & a World Without Rape,* made an impassioned yet sensible argument about why Polanski should be jailed despite my wishes.

> *. . . rape isn't just a crime against one person, and we don't prosecute it in order to fulfill any one victim's needs or wishes. Rape is a*

*crime against the social fabric that binds all of us together . . . when
the perpetrator goes unpunished, it makes all of us less safe. Not
just because there's one more rapist on the loose, but because that
lack of accountability sends a message to other would-be rapists:
Go ahead and rape someone. The rest of us don't care that much,
as long as it's not us or someone we love. In this case, we might add
a caveat: Especially if you're rich and talented and have powerful
friends.*

This is the reason, Friedman suggests, the plaintiff in any
criminal rape case isn't the victim—it's the government. Rape
cases are pursued by a representative of all of us because all of
us are harmed when someone rapes.

I do understand this. I also understand that the punishment should fit the crime. Polanski had already served time—
in both California *and* Switzerland. How much do they want?
And I struggle with why what "they" want matters. More strangers weighing in on my life!

The months of Polanski's incarceration in Switzerland, the
legal wrangling—it was all awful. The panic attacks and insomnia I'd suffered from on and off for my entire life returned in
full force. I was finding it harder and harder to concentrate at
work, and my boss, while understanding, was also concerned.
I was afraid I'd lose my job—which added to the insomnia and
panic.

As my advocate, Larry filed a "Victim's Statement" with the
appeals court supporting Polanski's motion to dismiss the case

against him. I think he cleverly combined my thoughts and wishes with a strong formal legal argument. Here is a portion:

> *Since the outset of this case, Samantha Geimer has attempted to be left alone. Because she is a victim of a celebrity crime, that has not happened. After years and years of being followed, pursued, hounded, photographed, and videoed openly and surreptitiously by hundreds, if not thousands, she was advised by a knowledgeable reporter that if she would only tell her story it would all go away. She was told that it was her silence that made pursuit of her even more intense. She told her story and she is still the victim of an intense public curiosity. Over the years, for example, her children have been approached at school, friends of hers have been approached for photographs or comments, surreptitious reporters and photographers have parked outside her house with drilled holes in vehicles attempting to take photographs or videos of her. Her children, in her absence, have been gifted by photographers for information—tell your child to throw away a gift toy. In violation of Judge Rittenband's order, the District Attorney consented to the making public of the grand jury testimony so that the world would know the sultry, [sic] albeit true, details of the crimes. It is now internetted for her husband, mother, and children to read.*
>
> *Anytime Polanski is in the news, Samantha's efforts to be left alone are vitiated. This happens when Polanski releases a new movie, when he is considered for recognition, i.e., an Academy Award. Samantha's life is significantly interfered with every time his celebrity becomes more public. It just happened again.*

On September 26, 2009, as the world knows, Polanski was arrested in Switzerland. That arrest has yet again focused a media frenzy on Polanski, and therefore on Samantha. Between Samantha and her counsel, they have received close to 500 telephone calls from media around the world seeking a comment, seeking interviews, seeking photographs, seeking appearances, seeking old photographs, seeking new photographs, seeking a statement, seeking anything to feed the frenzy. The response of "no comment" has been met with offers of money, and other gratuities in exchange for a word or two or an appearance from Samantha. The response has been: "leave me alone."

But they won't leave her alone. Her mother has been followed by news organizations and paparazzi. Samantha's children have been hounded by photographers and reporters. Samantha has been greeted at places where she tries to live her normal life, i.e., at an airport, with photographers, reporters, and paparazzi. They have surrounded her house waiting for the moment when she will yield to the pressure and come out and talk. Calls, at all hours, invade her at home, on her cell phone, and at her place of employment. The victim is again the victim. The pursuit has caused her to have health-related issues. The pursuit has caused her performance at her job to be interfered with, and has caused the understandable displeasure of her employer and the real possibility that Samantha could lose her job.

Now faced with economic consequences in this economy of being unemployed, yet once more this victim has been victimized. It has been happening for 32 years. Everyone claims they are "doing their job," but she may have no job. Everyone claims that they are acting to vindicate justice, but Samantha sees no justice. Everyone insists that she owes them a story, but her story continues to be sad. She endures this life because a corrupt judge caused, understandably, Polanski to flee. No matter what his crime, Polanski was entitled to be treated fairly; he was not. The day Polanski fled was a sad day for American Justice. Samantha should not be made to pay the price. She has been paying for a failed judicial and prosecutorial system.

This statement makes one more demand, one more request, one more plea: Leave her alone.

Whether you perceived Polanski as monster or the victim himself of vicious persecution, there is one thing both sides could agree on: the perfidy of my mother and me. In a piece in the *Huffington Post* that began, "I've had it with the Swiss," Joan Z. Shore, an expat living in Belgium who calls herself the founder of Women Overseas for Equality" ("WOE"—really), wrote:

The 13-year-old model "seduced" by Polanski had been thrust onto him by her mother, who wanted her in the movies. The girl was just a few weeks short of her 14th birthday, which was the age of consent in California. (It's probably 13 by now!) Polanski was demonized by the press, convicted, and managed to flee, fearing a heavy sentence. I met Polanski shortly after he fled America and was filming Tess *in Normandy. I was working in the CBS News bureau in Paris, and I accompanied Mike Wallace for a* Sixty Minutes *interview with Polanski on the set. Mike thought he would be meeting*

the devil incarnate, but was utterly charmed by Roman's sobriety
and intelligence.

Oh man. But this is the quality of insight that passes for journalism. He couldn't have raped that girl, because the thirteen-year-old was a skank, had been pimped out by her ambitious mom, and besides, all people who do bad things are stupid, ugly, and look like criminals. Shore doesn't let facts muddy her vicious judgment, but for the record, the legal age of consent in California is eighteen, and has been so for more than a century. Even in Shore's adopted Belgium, the age of consent is sixteen.

Perhaps the most disturbing slam from a Polanski apologist came in an October 2009 interview with Gore Vidal, conducted by John Meroney in the *Atlantic* shortly after Polanski was arrested. Vidal and Polanski had been friends in Hollywood.

> MERONEY: *During the time of the original incident, you were working in the industry, and you and Polanski had a common friend in theater critic and producer Kenneth Tynan. So what's your take on Polanski, this many years later?*
>
> VIDAL: *I really don't give a fuck. Look, am I going to sit and weep every time a young hooker feels as though she's been taken advantage of?*
>
> MERONEY: *I've certainly never heard that take on the story before.*
>
> VIDAL: *First, I was in the middle of all that. Back then, we all were. Everybody knew everybody else. There was a totally different*

story at the time that doesn't resemble anything that we're now being told.

MERONEY: *What do you mean?*

VIDAL: *The media can't get anything straight. Plus, there's usually an anti-Semitic and anti-fag thing going on with the press— lots of crazy things. The idea that this girl was in her communion dress, a little angel all in white, being raped by this awful Jew, Polacko—that's what people were calling him—well, the story is totally different now from what it was then.*

So I was a slut and an impediment to greatness to Polanski's supporters. How about his detractors? Well, if Polanski supporters thought I was a slut, Polanski detractors thought I was pitiable. As a makeup artist said to me before I appeared on ABC's *Good Morning America* to explain why I thought Polanski shouldn't be extradited, "Oh, you poor, poor thing." I know she was only trying to be kind, but was I a "poor, poor thing" because I'd been raped as a child? Was I still and forever to be a "poor thing"?

I told her I was okay, really. But I could feel her pity and didn't like it.

Here too Nancy Grace was particularly memorable. The blond vampire who eats misery for breakfast was positively gleeful at the time of Polanski's arrest. Polanski, she said, would "never see the light of day" again once he was extradited and sent away forever. Grace vilified his supporters and scoffed at the thought that there was any judicial misconduct in 1977, when she cross-examined Carmen St. George, a defense attorney, on her show in September 2009.

GRACE: *There was nothing proven about an irregularity. In fact . . . the only thing that we know for sure, is that Roman Polanski, a famous Hollywood director, admitted under oath he raped a 13-year-old. We know that much. . . . So you`re saying because the case is old, because he`s been living it up in a mansion in Europe, that we should just forget about it, that that's a problem, that Lady Justice should just pack her bag and go home?*

That's not what St. George was saying, but that didn't matter to Grace. Later in the show she spoke with Dr. Evelyn Minaya, a women's health expert.

GRACE: *Young ladies and women through all points in their life that have been raped as children. This is a child, a thirteen-year-old girl. It affects them forever.*

MINAYA: *Forever. And not only that, the physical aspects of it also. Remember, she had anal sodomy. Do you know that that puts her at an increased risk for anal cancer in her future, let alone all the other psychological ramifications that there are with that, you can just imagine.*

The show goes on in this vein. I was used to having my character maligned because of the rape. But now I was being told that because of the rape I was more likely to get cancer. Great. What's next?

I wanted to scream at the television, I am standing right here, I can hear you!

On another show, Grace referred to me as a "weak victim" who couldn't stand up for myself. She called herself a "victim's advocate." In other words, she needs a supply of victims to advocate for. No victims, no victims advocacy business. I can't help you here, Nancy Grace. I was the victim of a crime—I am, and always will be, a rape victim. But I'm not a victim as a person. I'm a strong woman who chooses to identify herself by her strengths, her interests, her family, and her loathing of gadflies who want to appropriate her life for their own purposes. I'm not available to you, Nancy Grace; go victimize someone else.

And then there was that other drama vulture, Dr. Phil McGraw. I read that he said I had a classic case of victim's guilt, and he'd like to help me. It's that kind of patronizing attitude that perpetuates rape victims thinking they *should* have something to feel guilty about. Dr. Phil, you're mistaking survivor's pride for victim's guilt. But there's no money in survivor's pride, is there? Thanks for the offer. I'll pass for now, but if I ever feel the need to get help from a TV host, I'll have my people contact your people.

· · ·

On July 12, 2010, after nine months of house arrest, the Swiss Justice Ministry issued a statement guaranteed to make Nancy

Grace's head explode: "The 76-year-old French-Polish film director Roman Polanski will not be extradited to the USA," the ministry said in a statement on Monday. "The freedom-restricting measures against him have been revoked."

I was so glad, because the last few months had worn me out. Now, I hoped, the press would stop hounding me. I could put my Rape Girl costume away, and go back to my wonderfully ordinary life—my family, my animals, my horror films. (Some people enjoyed Civil War reenactments; my family and I were more into Zombie Apocalypse reenactments on Halloween.) I was even happy that Polanski was being released, though staying in that nice house in Gstaad wasn't exactly Guantánamo Bay. It wasn't over though. The Los Angeles County DA's office continued bungling the case.

Before Cooley's epic failure, this scenario must have seemed a slam dunk. Switzerland had turned over other fugitives from American justice in the past, and this case was open-and-shut. Well, not exactly. For one thing, Switzerland has very specific criteria for extradition. People can only be extradited if they have six months or more to serve on their sentence back in their native country, and the court was not convinced that Polanski had six months to serve once he returned. Of course, no one knows—it was the ambiguity of the sentencing that sent Polanski skedaddling in the first place—but the Swiss authorities noted that Polanski likely wouldn't have more than six months because in the year Polanski was sentenced, not a single person in California serving time for unlawful intercourse served six months. In fact, few served more than two. Polanski was also in jeopardy because of his unlawful flight, but no one could predict what those sanctions might be. And even under California law, you can't be sentenced until you've been found guilty.

The main reason for Switzerland's refusal to turn over Polanski, however, was the DA's refusal to turn over key testimony. In January 2010, Roger Gunson—who had been having serious health problems—gave testimony under seal to be used in case he was too sick to appear in court. Polanski's team, as well as Larry and myself, wanted Gunson's testimony handed over, as we believed it would reveal key information about Judge Rittenband and judicial misconduct back in the 1970s. It wasn't clear how this might have affected the case, but I'm guessing it must have been pretty embarrassing to the Los Angeles County Superior Court.

Polanski's legal team complained that the DA's office was providing the Swiss authorities with "false and materially incomplete" information. Nevertheless, Los Angeles Superior Court judge Peter Espinoza rejected the defense lawyers' request to unseal the testimony—and that pretty much ensured Polanski's freedom.

Cooley was infuriated. "To justify their finding to deny extradition on an issue that is unique to California law regarding conditional examination of a potentially unavailable witness is a rejection of the competency of the California courts," he said in a press conference. "The Swiss could not have found a smaller hook on which to hang their hat."

Switzerland saw it differently. It looked like the United States had something to hide. It did. And it still does.

There were just two people involved in my rape in March 1977—the perpetrator Roman Polanski and me. I played my part—I was the kid who was raped. Polanski played his—he assaulted me, and was arrested and charged. And that should have been that. Still, even though I was only thirteen years old, I just knew this was turning into something far bigger than what happened that night. And somehow, what had happened, as bad as it was, was not going to be as bad as what was coming.

I hoped I was wrong. I must have been wrong, right?

Then I ran into the two-headed monster of the California criminal justice system, and its corrupt players whose lust for publicity overwhelmed their concerns with justice. To be fair, there are those who sincerely believe that laws must be enforced regardless of the consequences to the victims. For me, the consequences of the rape laws being vigorously pursued against Polanski would have meant I would be exposed to aggressive, damaging, and adversarial examination by Polanski's lawyers, who would make the case that either it never happened, or that I was some trampy thirteen-year-old temptress and so it wasn't that big a deal. My case would be tried not only in the court, but also in the media. All the stories about me would be salivated over again. My crime? Being the rape victim of a Hollywood celebrity. I realize that there are people who, in the pursuit of attention and notoriety, feel no shame. After all, the fame of both Kim Kardashian and Paris Hilton rests not on singing or dancing or acting, but on their ability to make a hot sex tape. I admire them for making the best of an uncomfortable situation, and if they can take the heat, then good for them. But it's not as easy as it looks.

. . .

Larry and my family agreed that protecting the victim—me—was more important than Polanski being prosecuted to the full extent of the law. We were forced to fight to allow him to plead to the least serious of the charges to avoid my being splashed across every tabloid in the nation. And then we had to fight again, recently, when without any consultation with me whatsoever, efforts were renewed to have Polanski extradited to the United States. And by the way, even in 1977 it wasn't a difficult decision. My family never asked that Polanski be punished. We just wanted the legal machinery to stop.

I was a young girl during the circus surrounding the rape in the late 1970s, and depended on the care of my parents and attorney. Now, thirty-five years later, I have my own judgment, developed over a long period of reflection, to guide me. Polanski made a horrible mistake and compounded it by fleeing the country. On the other hand, he has been publicly exposed as a rapist, his career has been damaged, and he has lived as an exile from the United States, the center of the movie universe. Enough punishment? There's disagreement on the answer to that. But to me it's the wrong question. I'm not interested in punishment; I'm interested in justice. And justice, I believe, starts with the interests of the victims—particularly when it is clear that the perpetrator is not a threat to the rest of society.

The brouhaha around Polanski's extradition has become ever more curious. There's simply no doubt that Judge Rittenband, the original presiding judge, was a shameless publicity seeker. DA David Wells has admitted to lying. Yet it appears that none of this will be investigated until Polanski surrenders.

I don't think that is the way our system is intended to work. We have a Department of Justice, not a Department of Punishment. We have Lady Justice, not Lady Punishment. She is holding scales; I believe these indicate balance. Not a balance between the rights of the victim and publicity for the judge. Not a balance between the rights of the victim and a license to lie by the DA. Not a balance between the rights of the victim and the ambition of a public servant. If there's to be any balance at all, it has to be between the rights of the victim (to end their suffering) and the interests of the state (to punish the crime), with the emphasis on protecting the innocent.

How can the state of California refuse to investigate the misconduct of a judge and a prosecutor, because a celebrity has broken the law? Shouldn't officials of the court be held to a higher standard? I call for the investigation of what happened behind closed courthouse doors in 1977 and 1978. As a victim, the California Victims' Bill of Rights provides me some consideration. But the district attorney's office refuses to extend any. Instead they unconscionably withhold those rights. They treat my rights as privileges that must be earned. And I earn them only by submitting. I must follow their unwritten rules, while they don't even follow their own laws. The offense they suffered at Polanski's flight supersedes all else. My rights as a citizen and a victim, the misconduct of court officials, those are set aside, because the rule of law must apply to Polanski first. Why? Justice applied selectively, applied at the whim of the district attorney's office. Why?

Punishing Polanski for what he did to me was only one motivation in many, and a relatively minor one at that. There were much more pressing concerns: politics, business, spectacle.

The analogy that always comes to mind when I think of the way I was treated is this: What if, instead of being raped, I were injured in a different way? Say I have a really bad cut on my arm that is covered by a bandage and that is just barely starting to heal. Would it be appropriate for anyone to say to me: *Wow, will you tell me all about how that happened? Can you take the bandage off so I can look at it? It's stopped bleeding, can you squeeze it a little so it starts to bleed again? Does it hurt worse now?* That's what it feels like to me, anyway.

The Polanski case was not a good, or even bad, example of justice. It was in some ways the opposite of justice. Justice is not intended for entertainment or the enrichment of public officials, pundits, and media corporations. I do not believe that punishment and spectacle can be substituted for justice. I do not believe that rules and laws for the sake of themselves are more important than justice. I do not believe that rules and laws applied in a vacuum for the sake of supporting a narrow point of view represent justice.

Because I am demanding justice for the victim, it would be hypocritical if I didn't also demand justice for the defendant. Justice equals fairness for all concerned. Polanski and I are human beings, not political footballs, and neither of us should be misused by the system. It may seem odd that I'm campaigning for justice for Roman Polanski, the man who was, for that sliver of time, so selfish and self-serving. But it's more bizarre to me that the system is such that, in this case anyway, the only way to get justice for the victim is to ask for relief from punishment for the criminal. It's not perfect. But it's right.

· · ·

In April 2013, the London Feminist Collective staged a protest of a retrospective of Polanski's films at the British Film Institute (BFI). Women marched with placards that said things like "Polanski's Still on the Run/But That Don't Bother the BFI None" and ran side-by-side photos of Polanski with Jimmy Savile, the knighted British entertainer, now deceased, who was recently found to have sexually molested hundreds of children. (Placard: "Would you run a Savile season?") The Collective released a press statement that said, in part: "The British Film Institute has joined in with the minimization of Polanski's crime by running a retrospective of his work without ever mentioning the fact that he is also a convicted child rapist [*sic*]. . . . The 'he's an artiste' defense arises every time these issues are raised and it remains utter garbage. Being an 'artiste' has never been an acceptable excuse for an adult male to abuse a child and it never should be."

This is a valid point, and of course I totally support it—who doesn't? I just don't want to be the anti-Polanski poster child, trotted out at anyone's convenience. For one thing, I still crave some measure of privacy, and would fight for any victim to maintain his or her own. For another, my case is too complicated and nuanced to make it a good example. I resent being appropriated for other people's campaigns and causes. If you're serious about accomplishing something good, start from a good place: secure the cooperation of those you want to help; don't exploit them.

A few days ago, I was on the YouTube website and stumbled upon a funny television commercial that happened to be directed by Polanski. It was a parody of a fragrance commercial, in which Natalie Portman and Michelle Williams, dressed as French courtesans, look like they're going to get romantic, and then get into a catfight over a perfume called "Greed." It was kind of like a dopey *Saturday Night Live* skit, and so I was about to just go on to something else, when sandwiched between the random commentary about the commercial was this: "The girl who claimed Polanski sodomized her is a liar and a fraud. So are those other two people who claimed the same thing in 2010." Nothing to do with the commercial. Nothing to do with anything. But it's like a Pavlovian response to the words "Roman Polanski." That response is either "He's a pedophile" or "She's a whore."

It is 2013, and I still find I have to steel myself whenever I see his name.

There is no end in sight to the controversy surrounding Roman Polanski. Partly it's because the tincture of time does not magically wash away the stain of rape. But also because there is no end to controversy about the act itself—what it is, when it happens, who gets to define it. The most intimate of human exchanges—sex, and its grotesque deviations, like rape—will be parsed and argued about forever. And political affiliations do not necessarily predict opinions about the subject. On *The View,* the very liberal Whoopi Goldberg famously argued that what happened to me might not be "rape-rape." I took no offense, but I had to laugh out loud. Oh my God, Whoopi, your audience is not going to be thrilled you said that! And they weren't. But even conservatives were offended when Republican stalwarts starting throwing around terms like "legitimate rape" and "honest rape" during the 2012 election season. As it turns out, rape is not an issue that lends itself to easy and predictable ideological analysis.

I cannot stop thinking, too, about the sexual norms of the 1960s and 1970s versus today. A *New Yorker* piece about the Horace Mann School abuse scandal I discussed earlier quotes Gary Alan Fine, a 1968 graduate and sociologist at Northwestern University. "This was the late sixties, and what we now think of as rape or sexual assault didn't quite mean the same thing in that age of sexual awakening,"

Fine said. "If you're a powerful person and you do things that others respond to because of your power, you may convince yourself that they really love you and this is between two equals." Love was not the issue in my case, but his point is well taken. The powerful are used to being wanted. They take it as their due.

In 2009, after the release of *Wanted and Desired,* Polanski wrote me this note.

Dear Samantha,

I watched Marina Zenovich's documentary for the second time and, I thought, I should write you this note.

I want you to know how sorry I am for having so affected your life. Watching you in the film, I was impressed by your integrity and your intelligence. And, you are right, they should give your mother a break! The fault was mine, not your mother's. I hope the pressure of the media has alleviated and that your family brings you much happiness.

Best wishes,
Roman Polanski

This note was written when Polanski had children of his own. Maybe being the father to a young teenager put the events of the film in perspective for him. It didn't change anything for me, but I could see the effect it had on my family, my mom in particular. It meant so much to them, and it was a relief to see them let go of some of that pain and anger.

In so many ways I've been a very lucky woman. For one thing, I was never taught that sex was bad—it was a natural thing you were meant to look forward to someday. Whether it was the permissive times I grew up in, the attitudes of my parents, or just my own nature—I never felt dirty or deeply ashamed because someone had sex with me against my will. I may have felt kind of stupid, but I never felt there was anything fundamentally wrong with me. This is not a small thing; for a rape victim, it may be a matter of life and death.

Recently I was reading about Elizabeth Smart, the girl who at fourteen was abducted from her Salt Lake City home, held captive in the mountains, and abused for nine months. When she spoke on a panel at Johns Hopkins University, she explained that one of the key factors in why she didn't try to escape her attacker was that she had been taught, through abstinence-only education, that she was worthless after being raped—that she was not fit to return to society.

"I remember in school one time, I had a teacher who was talking about abstinence," Smart told the panel. "And she said, 'Imagine you're a stick of gum. When you engage in sex, that's like getting chewed. And if you do that lots of times, you're going to become an old piece of gum, and who is going to want you after that?' Well, that's terrible. No one should ever say that. But for me, I thought, 'I'm that chewed-up piece of gum.' Nobody rechews a piece of gum. You throw it away. And that's how easy it is to feel you no longer have worth. Your life no longer has value."

I agree with Smart. As a society we're constantly giving young girls tips on how to stay safe: don't go out late at night, dress modestly, don't go out alone, don't drink, and don't have premarital sex. While I certainly understand why we tell women these things, and even think we can make certain commonsense choices that keep us from having sexual experiences we'll regret, we can't send the message that when something as grotesque as a rape happens, *you deserved it.*

The lasting effect of my experience with Polanski has not been trauma, whether psychic or physical. It's been a desire to maintain and nurture real connection—with friends, family, husband, even exes. (I'm friendly with everyone I've ever been involved with, I think—they're all like characters in the book of one's life, and you wouldn't want to put down the book without knowing what happens at the end!) And perhaps my experience has also created in me an empathy, and sometimes even a desire to reach out to women who have been the victims in highly publicized criminal cases. It pains me to think what they're going through, *besides* the actual experience of the crime. I remember, for example, hearing that the young woman who accused Kobe Bryant received death threats. *She* was the bad one for telling the police what happened?

This year I felt compelled to write to the sixteen-year-old girl raped by the two high school football players in Steubenville, Ohio. (I don't know who she is, of course; I sent it to her via Mike DeWine, the attorney general of Ohio.)

March 26, 2013

Dear "Jane Doe":

My name is Samantha Geimer, and in 1977, I was also Jane Doe. The massive media coverage surrounding you touched me and I wanted to reach out to you, understanding what is like to be at the center of a high profile rape case at a young age.

I was raped by Roman Polanski, just 2 weeks before my 14th birthday and ended up at the center of an intensely high profile case, that has followed me to this day, due to the nature of Roman's celebrity.

I just wanted to tell you that it gets better, that you'll be alright. Maybe not right away and maybe not all the time or all at once, but you'll move past this and be stronger for it. I remember how angry it made me to see and hear all the lies reported about me, all the lies about what happened, and even lies about Roman. It's hard to believe that so much of what you see and hear in the media can be untrue, but it is. I wondered why people with nothing at stake in it had such strong opinions and feelings about it. I felt used by the media, people making a living off of my misfortune.

It can be confusing, you know that it is not your fault, yet you may blame yourself for putting yourself in the wrong place at the wrong time. You know that the punishment those boys got, they deserved, but somehow you still feel bad to know that they are in jail. I have tried to find a balance. Knowing that the blame is not on me, it is on my rapist in a way made me feel somehow powerless. So I also can look back and realize while I made some unwise decisions that day, I shouldn't feel guilty or to blame. I feel less like a victim that way. That's just me though; you will find a way to fit all this awfulness somewhere in your life and get past it.

In the end, you are not a victim, you are a survivor. You are one of many and you are in very good company. Shame and embarrassment keep people from talking about these things; they let this kind of abuse hide in the shadows. You should know that your story shined a light on something people needed to see and talk about. Someone has learned something and didn't victimize someone else because of the publicity you have endured. And, for everything your family has been through, surely some good has come, to someone, somewhere, when another person perhaps hesitated and did not hurt someone else.

Mostly, I just wanted you to know that you are not alone. As this fades away to a memory of longer and longer ago, you are not alone. We survivors are many, and we are strong. Most important we are all around you and we all understand.

I hope that your future brings you many wonderful things; you don't have to let this drag you down. It will get better, and you will be okay.

Sincerely,

Samantha Geimer

CHAPTER 16

This book almost never happened. I was never moved to tell my whole story; I just wanted the story to go away. It wasn't that I hadn't thought about it. There were regular inquiries and offers going back to 1977. And there were times I was tempted. It would have been nice to have the money, and it would have been nice to have a pulpit to set the record straight. The controversy that's come in waves over the thirty-plus years of this story has caused enormous hurt and anxiety to me, and worse, to my family. To call more attention to us by writing a book about it was too painful to me and too abusive to the ones I love.

But then came Marina's documentary *Wanted and Desired*. The way she laid it out so simply and perfectly gave us a way to understand it all. Finally we could say, "That is it, that is the way it really happened." And after Polanski's arrest and the ensuing nightmare, my sons started seeing it in a different way. As boys, they may have been embarrassed by the attention; now as men, they were angry. They pretty much joined the rest of my family in now saying, "Okay, go get 'em." I was ready, too.

Every time I looked at an article or news feature or story about Samantha Geimer, I met a different person. There was Samantha the slut who used her charms to entice poor Roman Polanski into her web of perversion. There was the abused Samantha whose mother's ambitions were advanced by serving up her nubile daughter to the powerful director. There was Samantha the self-hating victim who apologized for herself and couldn't find anything wrong with her assailant. And there was Samantha the weak victim. I was never in front of the story; I was always reacting to the portrayal of one of these Samanthas.

Most of what my family, dear, brilliant, essential Larry, and I worked for in and out of court all these years was geared toward having privacy. Unfortunately, all these false Samanthas still leaked out. I was ready now to come out. Come out as myself.

The discipline of reliving the years—sometimes frustrating, sometimes sad—brought new insights, new understanding, particularly in terms of a greater understanding of Roman Polanski himself. As different as our lives have been, we do share a common sense of battle fatigue when it comes to the court system and the media. We've both been punished. We both want to move on.

We both might be considered victims. I can't speak for Roman; me . . . no thanks. The word *victim* comes from the Latin word meaning the person or animal sacrificed for some religious purpose. Over time it's developed to mean a person who suffers from an accident or incident that leaves them injured and compromised in some way. I imagine it must be terrible to be a victim.

I tell you this for one reason. It reminds me of one of the guiding principles of my life—one I wish I could share with all those who have called me a "weak victim." If you go through your life carrying hate in your heart, you really only hurt yourself. I didn't forgive him for him; I did it for me. Forgiveness is not a sign of weakness. It's a sign of strength.

AFTERWORD

by Lawrence Silver

Thirty-Five Years

Being Samantha Geimer's lawyer has been an interesting and rewarding challenge. When I started representing her, she was thirteen years old, and my mission was simple and clear: to keep her identity as a rape victim as confidential as possible. Samantha's parents believed anonymity was essential to her mental health, and that she must be allowed to lead a life as unaffected as possible by Polanski's criminal acts. That goal might have been realistic had the case ended in 1978. Even with Polanski's celebrity, the intense interest in Samantha likely would have totally faded. But that goal was never truly achievable once Polanski, quite understandably, fled the country after Judge Rittenband yielded to media pressure and reneged on the sentencing agreement. That flight gave the case (so to speak) legs. It led to thirty-five years of focus on Samantha and thirty-five years of my trying to protect her. At the outset, Samantha's family was not interested in pursuing Polanski in any civil litigation because, among other reasons, that would have meant revealing her identity. No amount of money from Polanski was worth that price.

But things changed. Polanski published a memoir in which he not only defended his illegal behavior, he sought to profit from it. Also, Samantha grew older and, although she still wanted to avoid attention, stronger. These factors contributed to the decision to proceed with the suit. While there were risks of disclosure, we could have the matter referred to a private judge and bring the action using an anonymous name, Jane Doe.

My role in this book has been quite limited. This is Samantha's story, but from just after the rape until now, I have been along for the journey. I have provided Samantha with information about the legal events, and helped jog her memory, especially of the early years. Remember, Samantha's recollection of those events, events still unsettling to contemplate, was that of a thirteen- or fourteen-year-old child.

Two items relating to the litigation were not discussed in Samantha's book and would, I think, be particularly interesting to those who've followed the case.

First, the photographs taken by Polanski on the day of the crime; and second, the recent amendment to the California Constitution which provides a victim of criminal activity with certain rights.

Photographs

After Samantha's mother made a police report, the police secured a warrant to search Polanski and his Beverly Wilshire Hotel room. Apparently after Polanski had taken some photographs of Samantha at Jacqueline Bisset's and Jack Nicholson's homes, he removed the used roll of film and put in a new one to take additional pictures. The police seized the camera with the unfinished roll still inside. The film in the camera was developed by the police department and printed. It's almost comical to consider now, but the police department's budget did not allow for the more expensive color processing. So you will see that two of the photographs in this book on pages 52 and 54 are pretty awful black and whites. The negatives had considerable shading that gives the color its rich quality. In black and white, they just look murky. The police never recovered the first roll of film.

In the civil litigation, I demanded all photographs of Samantha. Polanski turned over the prints from that previously unseen first roll of film. But I believed there were more. What happened was this: In executing the search warrant, the police didn't recognize the importance of a receipt/claim check from Sav-On Drugs' photograph department. Years later, I was told that Polanski gave his lawyer the receipt, and they secured the printed roll of film and negatives from the drug store. During the civil suit, his lawyer had to turn those photos over to me. These photographs, important both legally and historically, would likely have never been discovered if not for the civil suit.

Victims' Bill of Rights

In 2008 California voters adopted Marsy's Law, which amended the California Constitution to add a provision known as the

Victims' Bill of Rights. As described on the the California Attorney General's website:

Marsy's Law gives victims of crimes in California certain rights including:

1. *To be treated with fairness and respect for his or her privacy and dignity, and to be free from intimidation, harassment, and abuse, throughout the criminal or juvenile justice process.*

2. *To be reasonably protected from the defendant and persons acting on behalf of the defendant.*

3. *To have the safety of the victim and the victim's family considered in fixing the amount of bail and release conditions for the defendant.*

4. *To prevent the disclosure of confidential information or records to the defendant, the defendant's attorney, or any other person acting on behalf of the defendant, which could be used to locate or harass the victim or the victim's family or which disclose confidential communications made in the course of medical or counseling treatment, or which are otherwise privileged or confidential by law.*

5. *To refuse an interview, deposition, or discovery request by the defendant, the defendant's attorney, or any other person acting on behalf of the defendant, and to set reasonable conditions on the conduct of any such interview to which the victim consents.*

6. *To reasonable notice of and to reasonably confer with the prosecuting agency, upon request, regarding, the arrest of the defendant if known by the prosecutor, the charges filed, the deter-*

mination whether to extradite the defendant, and, upon request, to be notified of and informed before any pretrial disposition of the case.

7. *To reasonable notice of all public proceedings, including delinquency proceedings, upon request, at which the defendant and the prosecutor are entitled to be present and of all parole or other post-conviction release proceedings, and to be present at all such proceedings.*

8. *To be heard, upon request, at any proceeding, including any delinquency proceeding, involving a post-arrest release decision, plea, sentencing, post-conviction release decision, or any proceeding in which a right of the victim is at issue.*

9. *To a speedy trial and a prompt and final conclusion of the case and any related post-judgment proceedings.*

These rights would have made an enormous difference in Samantha's life, and in mine. They *were* in effect when Polanski was arrested in Switzerland in 2009—but just having these rights wasn't enough. Steve Cooley, the Los Angeles District Attorney at the time of the arrest, was preparing to run for California State Attorney General (he won the Republican primary, then was narrowly defeated in the general election). He led the campaign to have Polanski extradited. He announced that his office was not going to abide by certain provisions of the Victims' Bill of Rights. In addition, the courts, uncomfortable with the significant changes made by the Victims' Bill of Rights, seemed, at the least, reluctant to enforce them and even unsure how to go about it. This was the first major legal event where the victim was asserting her rights. Samantha was expressing the view that enough is enough. She sought, with the defendant, a dismissal of the action.

I believe it is crucial to the administration of justice to give victims rights, but it's not enough to just grant the rights; those rights must be enforced. It is important that the California courts acknowledge these new robust rights and enforce the Constitution consistent with the Court's own oath.

Samantha Geimer is whole now. But it was a sad day for American justice when Roman Polanski felt compelled to flee because of the clear judicial malfeasance. And it's been a series of sad days for Samantha because the judicial system has not fully, completely, and vigorously embraced and enforced the rights of victims.

ACKNOWLEDGMENTS

The journey of sharing a story I never thought I'd want to tell has been a long one. And only made possible with the help of strangers who became friends, friends who became family, and family who are my heart. I must acknowledge the contributions of the following:

Lawrence Silver is so much more than my attorney; he's been my protector, my collaborator, and my friend of thirty-five years. He has been there every step of the way. I've depended on his memory to tell my story, which in many ways is his story too. We are both deeply indebted to his assistant Wendy Lovgren, who has been invaluable to us both and to Mark Field, at Silver & Field.

Judith Newman, our cowriter, totally got me. She worked incredibly hard to help me put into words thoughts and feelings that had been percolating for so many years. She made what might have been a difficult process a pleasure.

Peter Borland is my dream of what an editor should be. He

always supported what my story meant to me and believed in having it told the way I wanted to tell it. His efforts allowed us to get it right. Special thanks to Atria's amazing publishing team, particularly Daniel Loedel, Felice Javit, Paul Olsewski, Diana Franco, Hillary Tisman, Isolde Sauer, Jeanne Lee, Jim Thiel, Dana Sloan, Lisa Keim, and Kimberly Goldstein—all led by my publisher, Judith Curr, who has been a true champion of this book from day one.

Christy Fletcher, Melissa Chinchillo, Mink Choi, Sylvie Greenberg, Rachel Crawford, the team at Fletcher & Company. And most especially my agent, Rebecca Gradinger. Rebecca gave me great guidance; she was instrumental in bringing the book to fruition, working hand in hand with everyone at Atria, and with me. Also, thanks to Kat Likkel, who was kind enough to send me to Rebecca, and to Craig Wolff, who helped get me started.

Retired assistant district attorney Roger Gunson. We weren't always on exactly the same side, but we never doubted his integrity and goodness. He really stood above the rest and was there when we needed him.

Marina Zenovich, who in her film *Roman Polanski: Wanted and Desired* told a sensational story with incredible clarity and brilliance. Her film gave my mother a measure of peace and closure, and for that my gratitude is deep and unending.

All of my friends, who protect me with their loyalty and sustain me with their warmth. Dawn McMillan, whose dedication and support has shown me what friendship truly means. Duncan Scrymgeour, whose incredibly kind heart is matched only by his intellect and wit. Michele Burke, my childhood friend: we got through those difficult years together, I don't know what I would have done without her. My friends from York who couldn't have realized back then how much I needed them. My friends from Hughes Jr. High who welcomed me, accepted me, and helped me pretend everything was normal when my world was falling apart. And a special few who were always there to listen with support and patience so I could talk it all out: Mark Atkins, Dudley Wilson, James Jennings, Patricia Budde, and Deborah Wolf.

My mother, Susan Gailey, who showed me how to walk through difficult times with my head held high. My sister, Kim, and Nana who taught me the meaning of family. Robert Nesbitt, our hero. My father, John R. Gailey, Jr., who gave me the refuge of a wonderful childhood.

And most of all, my husband of twenty-five years and best friend, David, standing by my side through so much, and my incredible sons, Jes, Alexander, and Matthew. I couldn't have done this without their encouragement. I wouldn't have done it without their support. And I wouldn't be here at all without their love.